1434 Essex St., #2
San Diego, CA 92103

Bible
Interpretations

First Series

July 5 - September 27, 1891

8-28-16
3:00 Phyllies plays
on Midway Concert
Navy Band

Bible Interpretations

First Series

John 1:1-18 to John 10:1-16

These Bible Interpretations were given during the early eighteen nineties at the Christian Science Theological Seminary at Chicago, Illinois. This Seminary was independent of the First Church of Christ Scientist in Boston, Mass.

By

Emma Curtis Hopkins

President of the Christian Science Theological Seminary at Chicago, Illinois

WiseWoman Press

Bible Interpretations: First Series

By Emma Curtis Hopkins

Managing Editor: Michael Terranova

ISBN: 978-0-945385-50-9

WiseWoman Press

Portland, OR 97217

www.wisewomanpress.com

www.emmacurtishopkins.com

LEE R. BAKER
1434 Essex St., #2
San Diego, CA 92103
619-962-9892

CONTENTS

Foreword

By Rev. Natalie R. Jean

I have read many teachings by Emma Curtis Hopkins, but the teachings that touch the very essence of my soul are her Bible Interpretations. There are many books written on the teachings of the Bible, but none can touch the surface of the true messages more than these Bible interpretations. With each word you can feel and see how Spirit spoke through Emma. The mystical interpretations take you on a wonderful journey to Self Realization.

Each passage opens your consciousness to a new awareness of the realities of life. The illusions of life seem to disappear through each interpretation. Emma teaches that we are the key that unlocks the doorway to the light that shines within. She incorporates ideals of other religions into her teachings, in order to understand the commonalities, so that there is a complete understanding of our Oneness. Emma opens our eyes and mind to a better today and exciting future.

Emma Curtis Hopkins, one of the Founders of New Thought teaches us to love ourselves, to speak our Truth, and to focus on our Good. My life has moved in wonderful directions because of her teachings. I know the only thing that can move me in this world is God. May these interpretations guide you to a similar path and may you truly remember that "There Is Good For You and You Ought to Have It."

Introduction

Emma Curtis Hopkins was born in 1849 in Killingsly, Connecticut. She passed on April 8, 1925. Mrs. Hopkins had a marvelous education and could read many of the worlds classical texts in their original language. During her extensive studies she was always able to discover the Universal Truths in each of the world's sacred traditions. She quotes from many of these teachings in her writings. As she was a very private person, we know little about her personal life. What we do know has been gleaned from other people or from the archived writings we have been able to discover.

Emma Curtis Hopkins was one of the greatest influences on the New Thought movement in the United States. She taught over 50,000 people the Universal Truth of knowing "God is All there is." She taught many of founders of early New Thought, and in turn these individuals expanded the influence of her teachings. All of her writings encourage the student to enter into a personal relationship with God. She presses us to deny anything except the Truth of this spiritual Presence in every area of our lives. This is the central focus of all her teachings.

The first six series of Bible Interpretations were presented at her seminary in Chicago, Illinois. The remaining Series', probably close to thirty, were printed in the Inter Ocean Newspaper in Chicago. Many of the lessons are no longer available for various reasons. It is the intention of WiseWoman Press to publish as many of these Bible Interpretations as possible. Our hope is that any missing lessons will be found or directed to us.

I am very honored to join the long line of people that have been involved in publishing Emma Curtis Hopkins's Bible Interpretations. Some confusion exists as to the numbering sequence of the lessons. In the early 1920's many of the lessons were published by the Highwatch Fellowship. Inadvertently the first two lessons were omitted from the numbering system. Rev. Joanna Rogers has corrected this mistake by finding the first two lessons and restoring them to their rightful place in the order. Rev. Rogers has been able to find many of the missing lessons at the International New Thought Alliance archives in Mesa, Arizona. Rev. Rogers painstakingly scoured the archives for the missing lessons as well as for Mrs. Hopkins other works. She has published much of what was discovered. WiseWoman Press is now publishing the correctly numbered series of the Bible Interpretations.

In the early 1940's, there was a resurgence of interest in Emma's works. , At that time, Highwatch Fellowship began to publish many of her writings, and it was then that *High Mysticism*, her seminal work was published. Previously, the material contained in High Mysticism was only available as individual lessons and was brought together in book form for the first time. Although there were many errors in these first publications and many Bible verses were incorrectly quoted, I am happy to announce that WiseWoman Press is now publishing *High Mysticism* in the a corrected format. This corrected form was scanned faithfully from the original, individual lessons.

The next person to publish some of the Bible Lessons was Rev. Marge Flotron from the Ministry of Truth International in Chicago, Illinois. She published the Bible Lessons as well as many of Emma's other works. By her initiative, Emma's writings were brought to a larger audience when DeVorss & Company, a longtime publisher of Truth Teachings, took on the publication of her key works.

In addition, Dr. Carmelita Trowbridge, founding minister of The Sanctuary of Truth in Alhambra, California, inspired her assistant minister, Rev. Shirley Lawrence, to publish many of Emma's works, including the first three series of Bible Interpretations. Rev. Lawrence created mail order courses for many of these Series. She has graciously passed on any information she had, in order to assure that these works continue to inspire individuals and groups who are called to further study of the teachings of Mrs. Hopkins.

Finally, a very special acknowledgement goes to Rev Natalie Jean, who has worked diligently to retrieve several of Emma's lessons from the Library of Congress, as well as libraries in Chicago. Rev. Jean hand-typed many of the lessons she found on microfilm. Much of what she found is on her website, www.highwatch.net.

It is with a grateful heart that I am able to pass on these wonderful teachings. I have been studying dear Emma's works for fifteen years. I was introduced to her writings by my mentor and teacher, Rev. Marcia Sutton. I have been overjoyed with the results of delving deeply into these Truth Teachings.

In 2004, I wrote a Sacred Covenant entitled "Resurrecting Emma," and created a website, www.emmacurtishopkins.com. The result of creating this covenant and website has brought many of Emma's works into my hands and has deepened my faith in God. As a result of my love for these works, I was led to become a member of Wise-Woman Press and to publish these wonderful teachings. God is Good.

My understanding of Truth from these divinely inspired teachings keeps bringing great Joy, Freedom, and Peace to my life.

Dear reader; It is with an open heart that I offer these works to you, and I know they will touch you as they have touched me. Together we are living in the Truth that God is truly present, and living for and through each of us.

The greatest Truth Emma presented to us is "My Good is my God, Omnipresent, Omnipotent and Omniscient."

Rev. Michael Terranova

WiseWoman Press

Vancouver, Washington, 2010

Lesson I

THE WORD MADE FLESH

John 1:1-18

Golden Text: The word was made flesh and dwelt among us. *"In the beginning was the Word."*

Augustine says that by this passage "John at once leads us to the topless mount of God." Jesus was the *"Word."* Christ was God. Jesus Christ was the word of God. Should God have any beginning as we reckon time? Should the word of God have any beginning as we reckon time?

Without beginning of years or end of days the word of God has dwelt in God, occupying all the Mind of God.

"In Him was all the fullness of the Godhead bodily."

Jesus means word or voice of God. Whoever speaks the word of God it is Jesus speaking, and whoever speaks all the word of God without mention or thought of any other word, he is Jesus Christ.

1

To know Christ is fullness of life. Christ is being spoken now. Many nations and tribes and people are proclaiming that to speak the words Jesus Christ spake is to show forth God.

"All things were made by Him; and without Him was not anything made that was made."

This writer, John, loved Jesus Christ, and so his love bore him into the bosom of Divine Mind where the perfect thought was born.

There is only God. But God — the true God — is not like any being described by mortal sense. God in Truth is One. The Word in Truth is God.

Mortal sense separates the word of God into many words, and the Son of God into many sons. But as there are no rays from the sun that lights our planet, but it is one only light, so there is One Only Son of God, One Only Idea of Mind, One Only Light of Spirit.

"All things were made by him," as all was *"Good,"* so there is *no evil.* Watch the way of Spirit and see Divine Goodness everywhere. Watch the way of God and see that there is no God like the being you have imagined, but Only One Great Vastness of Principle for you to use and use and use, making whatsoever things you please, but never "making" anything, for all that is Real is already *"made" as thought* in the *Mind Divine.*

"In him was life." Out of Christ there is no life. Even a grape cannot be manufactured by the physicist. Only Spirit is Life. All life is Christ, ever

2

living, never dying — hidden, by our manufacturing thoughts not true concerning Life, may be, but quickening, thrilling, vitalizing even whether we say so or not. Christ is the Only Life. Out of Christ — Truth, God, Righteousness is no life, only seaming of life. *"And the life was the light."* Life makes Light.

All the light of the sun will not quicken a dead eye to see the trees and grasses. But the living eye catches the light. A true word will make a living eye, for *the word is life.* The living mind catches the shining word of Truth and makes a quickening delight to all the people round about. Our word is ourself.

The living Spirit shines peace and health and harmony wheresoever it thinks its thoughts, *"Darkness comprehended* (overcame) *not."*

No claim of sense can quench the light of Truth believed in.

Every word of Truth is a pushing forth of the glory of spiritual life from us over the world.

"There was a man sent from God whose name was John."

Always we speak our bold John word before Jesus Christ shines forth from us.

Here at the God center where we dwell we know that our presence is to material beliefs as rebuking as John was to his age, till people listen indeed, then we are a glory unto them.

People listened to John. They heard his bold strong prophecies. Whenever we tell of punishments to come, or of delights to come, we are *"John."* For John told of futures. Jesus Christ tells always of *Now.*

"The true light, which lighteth every man that cometh into the World."

The murderer in his cell has this Jesus Christ *"Light"* in. him. The savage Indian has the *"Light"* of Jesus Christ shining within him.

If his darkness refuses the shining, yet this *"Light"* will burn his darkness quite away. All are safe. All are lighted by this quickening *Life Light.*

Shine on Word of God.

"He was in the world."

As Jesus Christ is to each man so is he also to the world.

Jesus Christ means *Word of Truth.* The word of Truth is Omnipresent. You can speak it anywhere. So you can *be* Jesus Christ any moment.

There is no moment when you cannot speak the whole word of Truth. There is no place where you cannot speak the whole word of Truth. This is the word *"in the world."*

"The world knew Him not." That is — externals, carnality, materiality, refuse to be swallowed, absorbed, lost in the word of Truth.

4

The word being spoken, however, in the midst of external surroundings compels all externals into submission.

For instance, in the midst of grief you say, Peace. This is Jesus Christ. Peace then reigns. You speak the word Peace as intensely as you felt the grief.

"As many as received him, to them gave he power to become the sons of God."

They who speak this word shall show their Godlike power, Jesus Christ was Power — is power — ever shall be power.

Those who speak the name JESUS CHRIST many times over find that they begin to show forth power. Then they demonstrate understanding of power. Then they are masters over all things.

The name in itself carries demonstration of all other words.

Demonstration is implied by the two words, JESUS CHRIST. Speak this name till its potentiality is in you, flows from you, satisfies you.

"Grace and Truth came by JESUS CHRIST."

There is no doubt about it. Truth is Omnipotence. So you demonstrate Omnipotence by this name. "Grace" is goodness. So you demonstrate goodness by this name.

"He hath declared him," The same idea is repeated here in another way. God-Omnipotence, God-Wisdom, God-Health, is declared by speaking

5

the name JESUS CHRIST till all the potentiality of the "God-head bodily" (or in demonstration) is shed abroad by you. This is *"The Word made flesh."*

July 5, 1891

Taken from the International Bible Lessons in the Christian Science Magazine, these were first printed in 1888, and for the first four years, written by Emma.

Lesson II

CHRIST'S FIRST DISCIPLES

John 1:29-2

Golden Text: Behold the Lamb of God which taketh away the sin of the world.

The golden text of this lesson is spoken by John. The outer world will always hear the word *"sin."* It talks of things bad and sinful continually. It looks and hopes for sin to be taken away. It has no idea that sin is only its mistake. It has not looked up the truth of the passage, "A man's word is his only burden."

So, whoever talks of sin made nothing, speaks much of kinds of sin, looks forward to cleansing, is the *John* type of mind.

The John type of mind, viz., the one who deplores sin — hopes for cleansing, adores a Savior itself, but is sure the rest of the people are opposed to Christ Jesus, begs them to "love Jesus," — is always upright, moral, rigid, making piety unattractive.

7

There is something divinely attractive in the impersonality of this manner of speaking which John showed.

He was the cousin of Jesus, but was not jealous of his superior understanding of spiritual doctrines or greater demonstrations of power.

Jesus and John had their eyes fixed single to the Principle *per se*, without mention of relationships, friendships, likes or dislikes, honor or dishonor.

Each Trusted the other. Neither attempted to teach the other. This is a great principle for us to learn. With the clear statement of doctrine (or Truth) before us, we must each see it our own way.

Both were martyred for their words. Jesus did not offer to save John from martyrdom. John did not offer to save Jesus. Each with grave majesty disdained to interfere with the other's methods.

"This is the Son of God."

John saw the Light of Eternity shine in his cousin's eyes. He was no personality to him, but the embodiment of Principle.

Jesus drew away two of John's disciples. One was John the beloved and the other was Andrew, who afterward pioneered in Russian wilds.

Andrew called his brother Simon Peter, and he also began to keep close to Jesus, *"Thou shalt be called Cephas, which is by interpretation, a stone."*

Cephas, or Stone, or Peter, was a special word of Truth upon which the church of Christ is founded.

Looking carefully into this mystery of Godliness we find that it is simply, that all who speak the words, which Peter spoke from bold conviction, are members of the church of Christ so visibly that they work his works.

The word which was the rock word was, *"Thou art Christ."* This is the recognition of Truth direct. Face to face John had said it to him. Peter said it to him. To see Christ face to face, is better than to be talking of him.

To speak directly to Principle with nothing between thee and Principle is to carry abundant evidence of your Spiritual power everywhere.

The best healing is done when we recognize the perfect nature of our neighbor. Our neighbor is Christ Jesus. If we see Christ Jesus in him we are of this church.

This recognition of the Jesus Christ in our neighbor *"taketh away the sin of the world."*

July 12, 1891

Taken from the International Bible Lessons in the Christian Science Magazine, these were first printed in 1888, and for the first four years, written by Emma.

Lesson III

ALL IS DIVINE ORDER

John 2:1-11

No place where Jesus preached, or day upon which He wrought a miracle, but what has divine significance. Nothing is by accident.

All is divine order. "Cana of Galilee." Cana is the closing of the circuit, or circle of Galilee. Here the boy attains His majority and publicly celebrates His own marriage to the ministry of the Holy Spirit.

The circuit is closed on the third day — the day of fulfillment — the marriage day. At Cana He is joined unto Spirit forever. The complete surrender of the soul to the way and will of the Holy Spirit is fitly symbolized by the happy marriage of His young friends on Wednesday. *The beautiful virgin to her beloved, Jesus to God. "Thy Maker is Thine husband."*

Jesus never wrought any miracle till He thus publicly closed His recognition of church and state and domestic authority over His speech and actions, and with only His mother for a witness solemnly pledged Himself to recognize as supreme the Inner Voice and the outer call of the Divine Spirit.

Two things He thus makes clear to the students of His teachings, viz: that He never condemned the institution of marriage, and that no unvarying success in miracle working may be looked for till there is complete surrender of the heart and hand and judgment to divine will.

Therefore, no matter how many multi-mental demonstrations one may make he does not indicate utter surrender to the spirit of God, except he from thenceforth show his dominion over all external conditions by bringing forth order out of what seems chaos, health out of what seems sickness, life out of what seems death, peace out of seeming discord. "Miracle" working is the sign of being absolutely united to Spirit.

"If I do not the works of the Father, believe me not."

How beautifully Jesus Christ sanctions true marriage. There is no scornful reproval — no insinuation against it. He spoke of the obligation of one man and one woman to be true and faithful to each other for ever and ever. He stamps His image on honorable marriage. He is the only speaker of ancient times, in the Bible or out of it, who speaks so plainly that there is no mistaking His meanings — *"They twain,"* and "twain" means *two.* Paul's

12

words can easily be construed to mean another way. John the Revelator never carries the intimation of reverence for marriage in spite of his using it for a figure.

David's ideas are repulsive. But Jesus Christ — no wanton wandering from the plighted troth — no infidelity to the vows spoken to bind us to be faithful forever can we find excuse or sanction for in His teachings.

He or she untrue to the marriage pledge cannot expect the power of the Holy Ghost to work miracles thru him. It was at this pledging time that Jesus wrought His first miracle.

The Spirit bore witness with Him that He was ONE with it. This marriage "in Cana" was the outward picture of the primal union or marriage of Jesus Christ with Spirit.

Madame Guyon sought to be married to God. She succeeded in catching glimpses of this union several times, but she accused God as sending so much evil upon those united unto Him that her words made a cloud of darkness perpetually between herself and that "Maker who is thine husband." There is wine and mirth and friendly joy in marriage with God-Spirit. *Wine* is a word signifying *reviving, refreshing joy*. They who know Jesus Christ indeed, drink refreshing, reviving, invigorating words. The refreshing, reviving, invigorating words Jesus made the wine of, wine praises of the goodness and tenderness and bounty of God.

How perfectly He demonstrated that He was actually in love with Spirit by immediately doing the works of God! After this celebration of His own eternal Oneness with God, He could restore a palsied hand to vigor in an instant. He could call the living to come forth out of coffins and graves. He could make bread and fish self-increasing. He could coin gold on the instant for meeting all current expenses. He did not believe in owing even the proud government of Caesar anything. *"Render unto Caesar the things that are Caesar's."*

Unless we can do all the works that He did we have not closed in with the old ways at Cana and started the circuit of Galilee in Spirit. "The same works that I do shall ye do."

The "works" He did, we realize, were all accomplished by His knowing that when one came to Him drooping in body it was the outward picture of a drooping hope. When one came in consumption it was the outward picture of a hope departing or consuming. He could see that a word would quicken the hope — would restore the hope.

Looking into the mind realm where the thoughts were dwelling, a meek little woman, who understood Jesus, saw that a young man's hope was failing. What hope was it that was failing? The hope that he might be a success among men. The people said his nerves and muscles were failing. She saw his hopes drooping. She understood, because she understood Jesus Christ well, that there is no hope ever stirs within one of us but that God hath for us the actual fulfillment of that hope.

So she told him by silent ministry akin to the invisible marriage ceremony of Jesus Christ, that truly God would fulfill his expectations. Then aloud she said: "You will be successful, child." This was the "Wine" he was waiting to drink. It was the Word of God. "Thy words were found, and I did eat them and Thy word was unto me the joy and rejoicing of my heart." So he was well from that hour.

This is the power of prophecy. "Prophecy is mine and sound judgment." They can tell of good to come who have united with the Spirit that is Divine

Goodness all bounty without lack or failure. Whoever believes in weakness has not yet come into Cana. For Jesus Christ teaches that the truly joined to Spirit are filled with Omnipotence: "All power is given unto Me in heaven and earth."

Whosoever believes in sickness is not united unto Spirit, for Jesus Christ was explicit and definite, "heal the sick." Do not leave people in their sickness. Do not accuse God of sending sickness.

"As I live, saith the Lord, I know my thoughts and I think towards you thoughts of peace and not of evil, to bring you an expected end."

The end we all expect is good unto ourselves. We deeply and profoundly love prosperity and peace and health. These we have a right to and nothing else.

"Woman, what have I to do with thee?"

"Gracious lady! Keeper of my past; now I am listening for the voice of the Spirit. She does not yet bid me act."

So He broke away from the ways of Galilee's former hastenings, and without doing anything, did all things speedily. With the power of Spirit hastening through us there seems to the world delay, but all the world's armies of power and learning could not overtake our ministry if we are truly joined to God. *Festina Lente.*

All who obey the voice of Sophia (the Spirit) heed not the ways of the guests at the marriage, yet they do satisfy their hearts fair hopes. Then even the great ones at the former marriage obeyed Him. So it is always promised to the spiritually minded that they shall have "Kings come bending" and all the earth shall be theirs.

Notice that a woman, a "Gracious lady" recognized that He was great in Spirit. Cadijah recognized Mahomet. So "Woman" shall always know when the voice of the Spirit is speaking. And she shall tell the world what is true of Jesus Christ; also what is true of you and me.

"Six water-pots of stone." Here is our lesson for today put so plainly that he who runs may read. When Jesus Christ demonstrated the power of Spirit He always took the materials at hand such

as they were; He did not take any loaves and fishes except such as they had on hand to look up and praise God with and feed the multitudes.

He took Lazarus just as He found him. He took the "Six stone water-pots" and water they had at hand. Nothing else. This signifies that you are to take your rough circumstances, your bodily conditions, your human affairs, just as they are and holding them in your mind give thanks and bless the providing Jehovah that within them is the wine of peace and success and health. This giving thanks and praising God the down-bending Spirit for the wine of joy and goodness, surely contained within your circumstances the stone water-pots of your affairs just as they are, is the silent transmuting potency of Jesus the Christ.

A man who takes his last copper pennies and looking up to heaven gives thanks, is doing that action which is the key turning into re-enforcements of Jehovah laid up for him from the foundation of the world. The copper pennies are all he needs to work with. The stone jars are your own affairs. They are just what is given you to manage with to show how powerful the Spirit is in dealing with you for your increasement.

Archimedes said give him standing place and he would move the world. But Goethe was more like Jesus Christ by saying, "Make good your own standing place, and move the world."

Jesus Christ said He would lay down His body and take it up. Moses took his own rod and made it a serpent; his own hand and made it leprous with a thought; his own hand and healed it with a thought.

The queen was surprised that they had such dirty rags in a rich paper mill. But soon the manufacturers sent her some shining white paper made from those same rags. So by this lesson you may learn that you do not need one single thing to do with more than you already have if you know the law of praise and thanksgiving. At a faith-cure meeting a man kept praising God that he was so well, while a great tumor or some other kind of swelling was plain to be seen by his neighbors. This was his "stone water-pot." But he praised God publicly that he was so well for a whole fortnight. Long before the fortnight was up he was well, so that even his neighbors could see it so.

Take the home as you find it, child, and turn it into a home indeed by praising God that there is a Spirit of Goodness working with you and through you and by you and for you to make all things well.

Take your business as it is, child, and praise Divine Love that there is a strong, wise way out of your dilemma. Take your professional hopes, your children, your work — nothing can be more common than stone water-pots — and set them right by praising the Spirit. Praise is the "wine" of daily experience. The praise of Divine Love — the Motherhood of God is the plenteous wine of Cana of Galilee.

July 19, 1891

Lesson IV

JESUS CHRIST AND NICODEMUS

John 3:1-17

There is always, amid the formal sectarianism of the most formal and sectarian body of people, one who is "A Man of the Pharisees named Nicodemus." That is, by reason of his being called upon to teach, and being in some way a leader among his colleagues, he has found himself unconsciously concluding that there are finer meanings and deeper intentions in religious precepts than he has been taught.

Mind always puts out tendrils and lays hold on new meanings if it is not willfully set to a prejudice. The mind that makes God its theme will sooner or later meditate much on Jesus Christ, unless it is the mind of one determined to gratify bodily passions. Jesus Christ draws the mind that thinks on God as a magnet draws a steel filing. "No man cometh unto Me save the Father that is in Me draw him." We are drawn to those who have a quality akin to something within ourselves. So Nicodemus was drawn to Jesus.

There is some great idea that your mind has been meditating upon, some principle not definitely understood by you, but which it is possible for you to understand perfectly. You ought to get acquainted with that idea. You notice, don't you that in all the pauses of the business or conversations of the day, the vague but great idea comes up? So Nicodemus had for days been looking towards the idea of the power of faith as the prophets of the past had demonstrated it, and as the young man traveling about the country was demonstrating His principles. How did it happen that Elijah raised to life the Zarephath child, was fed by ravens, had such prophetic powers? How did Elisha raise the boy to life, heal the waters, cure leprosy? Was it not by the presence and working of the same God that he, Nicodemus, worshiped? Why should not this God work miracles now as in the old days? Surely God had never departed as the health of His people, the strength of their life, and the answerer of their prayers, yet nothing was done as in days past. Why not?

Maybe the young Jesus was right. He would go and see. He had been a moralist, Nicodemus had, and taken pride in his morality. So he came to Jesus, High moral conduct, coupled with thoughts of God, is liable to strike the white heat of goodness as Christ quality.

Jesus Christ preached His most stupendous doctrines to audiences of one and two. He taught over and over again not to despise the smallest circumstance or opportunity. "The situation that hath not its duty, its ideal, was never yet occupied by man." James Holmes found at Castle Bar an audience of three to hear him where he had been publicly announced to preach. Instead of shutting his mouth he opened it and preached so earnestly that one of the three, a young man, was converted, and was afterwards called the "Tongue of Fire" because he was so fervent in Spirit.

Jesus Christ waived the personal praise. He never received it from anybody who revealed His Being among them as another man with just a few points of ability, perhaps, above the usual Rabbi. Praise of His teachings He received. Praise principle, not person. Do right because it is right, and not through fear of somebody or love of somebody. So He drove straight to the need of Nicodemus: *"Except a man be born again, he cannot see the Kingdom of God."* "Nicodemus, except a man look into the Spirit only, utterly refusing to call any man of flesh or any earthly circumstances, his environment as help or hindrance he cannot set his home life, his health, his affairs, or his neighbor's health and affairs into harmony."

How coarsely Nicodemus answered Him. The mathematician responded to the entranced musician concerning the marvelous music, "Yes, it was wonderful to see the violinist move his elbow so many times in a minute." So, "The natural man receiveth not the things of the Spirit for they are foolishness unto him and he cannot know them, because they are spiritually discerned."

But Jesus Christ understood the law of mind. He knew how to hold the concentrated attention of His hearer till he should understand that *"Never the Spirit was born, the Spirit shall cease to be never; end and beginning are dreams."* He knew that it must be by the recognition that all power whatsoever is of the Spirit and not of intellect or physical force: "Except a man be born of water and of the Spirit." The Rosetta Stone to all miracle-working is that lesson on the increasement of loaves and fishes. The Rosetta Stone to this birth of water and Spirit is the statement, "If any man will come after Me, let him deny himself."

Now He never taught that we should deny the good in ourselves; certainly He meant that we should deny the evil. He told His hearers that it was His words of which He was speaking and the power of His words, so we know that the baptism of water of which He spoke to Nicodemus was the use of the washing words of denial, whereby the mind that has thought things not true is cleansed of its errors, as a body is cleansed by water.

There were certain errors or mistakes called profitless and nothingness and uselessness by Him, serving to hide the power of the Spirit. To deny these errors is to call them by name and re-ject them. This is the water baptism this great metaphysician meant. Now Naaman's seven washings in Jordan were typical of the seven denials every mind must make to be cleansed of error. By looking them over we know exactly what errors to reject and what to eschew.

The first washing we do must be the rejection of the belief in another power operating in the universe besides omnipresent, omnipotent, omniscient Goodness. There is no power of evil. This denial is the washing away of evil imaginations, so that we do not any more believe in the possibility of any cruelty or greed or crime coming nigh us forevermore. According to the law of mind action, we find that it sets the world free from evil also.

The second washing we must do is the speaking of the positive Word of rejecting the belief in another substance than Spirit. If God is omnipresent Spirit, then indeed Spirit is the only substance present anywhere; so the rejection of the supposition of the reality of matter is a necessary process. Matter has no reality, or, there is no matter. This Word of denial has the effect of cleansing us from as much experience of the hindrance or burden of matter as the law of the Word brings, spoken as an experiment or in faith. You certainly do find the hard tumor, the stiffened joint, or the heavy indebtedness grow less. This second washing is very, very efficient in making hard ways easy and heavy burdens light, exactly as the personified Word of truth promised that it should.

23

The third washing Word (remember that Jesus Christ was always teaching words and thoughts and states of mind by material terms) is the denial of our false notion that there is any life, substance or intelligence in matter, for if there is no matter surely God is the only life, Spirit the only substance, Omniscience the only intelligence.

An enchanting freedom comes with the third washing enjoined by Jesus Christ. The mind throws off the ugly nightmare of its third delusion by boldly announcing that there is no life, substance, or intelligence in matter. The heart rises with quickened hope. The friendship and beauty and goodness of living we see. The mind is clear to understand what is reasonable and right. Knowledge of Truth is freedom. Gautama Buddha and Jesus Christ both said so and proved it.

Take the fourth washing Word boldly. Naaman hesitated and was petulant. We will press boldly forward for the mark of the high calling of Regeneration, which is the subject of this lesson. By this time you see that Regeneration means giving your spirit perfect freedom.

The fourth Word of self-denial states that as matter is not a reality its sensations are fallacious. There are no sensations in matter. This Word will cause pain to falter and fail; will cause sensual appetites to fall away. We have no taste, sight, or hearing but for Spirit. "Taste and see that the Lord is good." "Feel after Him."

The fifth washing is a severe one for some of us to take, but there is no escaping the metaphysical meanings of Jesus Christ. Sin, sickness and death are delusions. This does not make a stealing or a slaying good, but announces that they are delusions, without power to hurt or hinder. The temptation to falsehood, the inclination to transgression, are unreal. To know this sets us free from them. Sickness and death are a myth.

Can Spirit be diseased or die? Since God is spirit, the only Substance, the speaking of this washing Word of denial is the sure setting free from sin, sickness and death.

These five cleansing waters are suitable and essential for all the world. There are two special ones applying to each man, woman, and child, besides the five for all the world. You can easily find out what two you ought to make for yourself.

There was once a woman who loved money so much that she saw everybody through her thought of money. If she looked at you she thought first of how much you were worth, or how much she could make out of you. You see by her looking at everybody and everything through money eyes, she got blind — quite blind. Money is blinding. If she wanted to see clearly she should deny herself of looking through money. It would be well for her to say much, "There is no money in Spirit."

A child's toothache will depart if you say, "There is no pain in Spirit." Your burden of poverty will clear off if you say, "There is no poverty in Spirit."

There are many who look at their acquaintances and friends and all circumstances through jealous ideas of some sort. They unconsciously or consciously wonder how much of their own rights, or position, or possessions, the other will get away from them. So they have lost one or more of their faculties, for jealousy is cruel and lops off from us our fondest hopes. Such should deny themselves of looking and judging through jealousy. Let them say, "There is no jealousy in Spirit."

Notice that this lesson reads that we must be cleansed by water and clothed by Spirit. Jesus gave the idea that we should take the house, swept and garnished, and fill it with good "Spirits." "Spirits" are words, as *"My Words are Spirit."*

There are seven Words of affirmation that are the hot glory of God over and through all who make them. Ye came forth from God. "No man upon earth is your father." Thus these Words are the shining forth of your own nature with which you were endowed from the great Forever without beginning of years or end of days. None of the miracle-working power Nicodemus wished to be master of is ours till we have boldly announced the spiritual nature and office we are endowed with.

This is the first affirmation of Spirit: Life, Truth, Love, is God. Then we recognize all Life as God and all Truth and all Love as God. We hail and welcome and praise all the living Beauty, all the living Strength, all the living Kindness; we recognize, knowing that it is God.

This recognition of Good is the shining forth of our own Goodness. Once it was thought that we were able and capable if we recognized vanity or deceitfulness in a neighbor, but now we know that since vanity and deceitfulness are nothingness and profitless, that it is a waste of time on the insubstantial. That which we see of Good is our own thinking or our own shining forth of our own Spirit. We learned by last Sunday's lesson that everything has the potentiality of Good ready to increase itself by our praise and blessing.

The second Word of Spirit is: "I am the idea of God, and in God I live and move and have my being." As God is omnipresent, we move safely and boldly on. This "spirit" or Word of the I AM makes us bold and joyous. All is joyous in spirit.

The third is: "I am Spirit, I am Mind; I shed abroad Wisdom, Strength, Holiness." Such a fire baptism as this Word radiates or reflects from us over the world to make people wiser, stronger, holier where we are, is only brought to pass by this affirmation, or "Yea, yea," of Christ.

The fourth baptism from above is our announcement that God the Spirit works through us to will and to do all things well. This is our Word from above, or birth from Spirit, that makes us efficient in healing and helping all with whom we come in contact. The old ways of depreciating our words and our works are done away with. We now

27

rejoice in our efficiency, since we know it as God the Good doing all things.

There is the fifth Word from above that secures our immunity from sin, sickness, and death, and that makes all the people secure when we come near them. Like the fifth denial, the fifth affirmation takes strong rising "To do the will to prove the doctrine."

I am governed by the law of God, and cannot sin, nor suffer for sin, nor fear sin, sickness, or death. As spirit we cannot swerve from our orbit any more than a star in its course. To swerve and falter would be sin, but Spirit cannot sin for God is Spirit. "He'll surely guide our steps aright." There is the safe walking of all who speak these Words through all the thorny ways of delusion.

Then the two "Other Spirits" or Words of affirmation, which belong to each of you, you must find out for yourselves. Notice that Paul says that in his greatest weakness is his strength. So you can see that if you have believed yourself inefficient or ignorant you must let the Spirit of Truth drop down over you with the bold affirmation: "I am strong and efficient. I praise the Spirit that now works with me and through me and by me and for me to do all my work faithfully and well.

"I am wise with the Wisdom of Spirit." This is the full potency of the treatment Jesus gave Nicodemus. "Marvel not." Only the carnal intellect marvels, wonders, asks questions. Spirit knows.

So Nicodemus rallied his faith. He had entered the presence of Jesus with hope. Hope is only the left hand; faith is the right hand. "Hope thou in God." Have faith in the Good. Your faith will show forth; your works of good faith will be good when you have learned how to be born of water and of Spirit according to this meaning of Jesus.

July 26,1891

Lesson V

CHRIST AT SAMARIA

John 4:5-26

The reason for keeping the Bible records is because they describe the religious experiences of
every mind under each class of circumstance recorded. Every mind has its religious aspiration,
which is its perfume, as every flower has its perfume.

Political history teaches ethics, fixing the mind
on the results of injustice, justice, oppression, lib-
erty, as carried on by civil authorities.

Material history teaches what can be done
with materiality. The silver cup lost by a workman
in a jar of acid, precipitated by Faraday, re-made
by the silversmith, satisfies us that we need not be
utterly bereft of silver cups, though they seem
utterly gone. The Bible records use no meaningless
or unnecessary terms, Jesus Christ means Word of
Truth, or Child of God. The religious aspirations of
each mind is its Jesus Christ idea — it's Word of

absolute truth. The mind is a kingdom or realm of thoughts. The most powerful, the oldest, the noblest, is its highest Word of Truth, or Jesus Christ. "Come and reign over us, Ancient of Days."

Thus the walk of Jesus Christ through this realm of carnal or earthly experiences is at each step of His going a living teaching of what to do under all the kinds of experiences we each have, in order to show forth Jesus Christ, or "Let the same Mind be in us that was in Christ Jesus."

Here is the lesson of what to do when we have been trying to be good and true for a long period, and as nothing seems to come out of it we are tired and discouraged.

We have been told positively by the spiritually-minded of every age that:

"If we will strive to be good and true,

To each of us there will come an hour,

When the tree of life will burst into flower,

And rain at our feet a glorious shower

Of something grander than ever we knew."

But though we have striven faithfully we are the most burdened and unfortunate of anybody we know.

Jesus Christ took up all our experiences on purpose, and in the midst of every one of them He spoke those Words, which we must speak under like circumstances. Here He took up the weariness and discouragement of our good motive when it sees no fruits in prosperity. He "sat thus on the well."

Do you remember the lesson He gave of what to say when you have had nothing to eat for a long time from any cause whatever? Do you remember what Words He told us to speak when physical anguish and the desertion of friends have broken our hearts?

Well, in the same fashion He tells us what to do when exhausted, discouraged, disheartened with the struggle to succeed. He sat thus on the well in Samaria. Samaria means watch post, or posted notice. Perhaps there is nothing that will mark itself on your face or give your whole character away to your acquaintances like what you choose to do when a turning point or crisis of thinking is reached by your mind. There comes a time when the blooming matron is called an old lady. This point just reached is Samaria. If the man or the woman can realize just the instant of weariness of the whole way of thinking and living and sit deliberately down and make the right resolve, a noble look will steal over the face of the young man and a new beauty will illumine the woman's.

Once a woman caught the gleam of this rest on the well of Samaria all in a flash and that which we are now carefully repeating was told to her from on high. So she sent out this word to all who would hear it. When you are disheartened and heart sore with the journey of your best efforts through this strange world, sit down and rest for the prayers you have prayed and the true Words you have said to be unto you a well of Living Water whose best draught you are about to drink, as Jesus announced the most refreshing doctrine He had ever put forth from the well of Samaria upon which He rested. When you have done the best you could, seemingly all to no purpose, put on your best clothes and sit down to wait for the heavenly guest who is to pass over your threshold that day.

This is the time when you are to "Rest in the Lord and He shall bring it to pass." So a poor, tired, little mother with her hungry children clinging to her knees, deserted of her husband, friends insisting that if she had done differently things would have been different, while she was doing her very best, obeyed this message and rested to wait for the heavenly Good that must come to her that day. And the Good came. This is a working principle to go by. In the science of mind or metaphysics as taught by Jesus Christ we are taught all those Words of Truth which are Everlasting Arms underneath, or the well of Living Water upon which we may rely for each part of our journey.

For instance, suppose that you have been told that God, the Divine Principle of Goodness, is your sure Health, and according to the law of prayer, or affirmation of Truth, you have daily and hourly spoken the words, "God is Health: no sickness or disease can get any hold on this Health, which is

God. Yet sickness and disease do seem to have a hold upon your health, and you are disheartened. Do not force yourself to speak the words then. Rest, wait. The True Health Thought is bending over you. Soon it will descend. This is the moment of fruition.

Far in the Oriental past they taught that the flower of Truth blooms in the Silence after the storm and stress of effort.

This is the time when, if you speak or work or struggle, you must start the work over again.

An innocent man, condemned to be hanged, says faithfully, "I am innocent. I trust in my innocence to defend me. Innocence is a wall of defense. Innocence is God. "You cannot hang me I defy you." Yet he stands on the scaffold. There he stops for pure weariness, the long night watches spent in this prayer of innocence. They cannot hang him. The words of Truth are sure. He does not look to the people to defend him. People always fail us. He does not look to the law books to show his cause just, for the law books are double-minded. But he trusts Omnipotent Principle.

So if the event has hung long and heavily over your home and you have faithfully declared God would loose the clutch of the trouble, you must cease from prayer at Samaria and "Trust in the Lord, for He shall bring it to pass." The Lord is the Law of the Good made manifest.

The fact that Jesus spoke to the woman of low origin in Samaria, the low shows that the most trivial circumstance of daily transaction is to be dealt with exactly as the most momentous.

If in making a garment it does not come out right after your hardest efforts — rest, wait. Now you will do it perfectly. When looking for a situation, if you become tired or disheartened — rest, wait, no matter what the contingencies may be. Weary discouragement is the "Hail to Thee" of Samaria reached. Here is an offer better than you imagined, "I that speak unto thee am He."

You who have been battling for your life with noble words such as the Science teaches concerning the impossibility of the clutch of death upon the life that is yours omnipotent, give up at Samaria and see how quickly the Living Water will now spring up within you.

As Jesus Christ walked among the lowly so let this Principle guide you through every vicissitude, great or small:

"Christ dwelleth not afar

The king of some remoter star,

But here among the poor and blind,

The bound and suffering of our kind."

The woman pointed to the mountain Gerizim, in plain sight, where the very same lesson was taught by Abraham's giving up the tension as to his offering, all that he had to the Lord, trusting utterly.

All the ages have had their ministers of this Law of Life: that there is a sure Helper near every man, woman, and child, who will bring everything to pass for us when we give up the expectation of getting help from any other source.

"I will lift up mine eyes unto the hills from whence cometh my help. My help cometh from the Lord, which made heaven and earth." Give up the tension. The eagle ceases from flapping his wings, and yet on and up it soars with folded pinions, resting in the Law.

The mountain unto which we look is the memory of the highest thought we have ever thought, or the highest Word that now comes into our mind. Jesus Christ said that this was the worship in Truth and in Spirit.

Whatever is true of Spirit is true. In Spirit all is good. Thus when we speak of evil we are not speaking Truth, for only that which is true of Spirit is true at all. This is the only worship of God that is acceptable. *"I am God and there is none beside."* God is Spirit. Thou art my all. There is no higher Truth we can speak than THOU art my all.

Whoever rests securest in this statement is manifesting Jesus Christ most. To him we go for help as we go to a spring for water instead of going to a sand bank.

The quality of your faith makes the quality of your ministry. If you believe in God as your support, do not stop short of the highest faith of Jesus Christ, who made the fish precipitate the gold within his being to pay the civil tax. Faith is the alembic wherein the right Word is crystallized that makes you master over every situation. Neither in this place nor that place, neither for one alone but for all.

If you trust in the goodness of the Divine Law working for you and believe that all things are made ready for you, you cannot but be a well of trust, a mountain of good faith to which the doubting and hungry come and dip in their cups for your ministry. Stand boldly by your faith; "I that speak unto thee am He." The saving-from-poverty thought is the confidence in God as your only supply. There have been people who prayed till they arose from praying and found money on the table or in their purse to help them. Then they were ashamed to hold on to the words of acknowledgment that God had indeed shown forth through them exactly as in Jesus Christ. Did He not say, "Where I Am there you may be also?" Why should we not be in the Spirit of Truth enough to believe that "All things are possible with God?" How many who read that wonderful little blue magazine* were ready to believe that the Spirit had helped those people as recorded in it?

Why even those who realized the manifesting power of the Word of faith were hiding the copy, which told of miraculous answers to prayers.

If one believes in the bounty of God, keep close to him for you may dip your empty cup into his full waters of supply and by a metaphysical process catch the Prosperous Mind. If one believes in God as his unfailing Health, keep close to him for that metaphysical process which is like the outer air cleansing the air of a room when the window is opened, so may you catch Health from his Spirit of Health.

Good, all Good is yours by divine right. How well your deep heart knows this. It is your Jesus Christ thought. Hold fast to It. "I Am He — thy Savior from poverty, misfortune, pain, trouble — I Am Messiah." Come boldly up to that high thought in your mind. Trust it. Your highest thought is that one which if it reign over you, will make you glad, strong, vigorous, healthy, prosperous. It is your Savior — Messiah. Not to come, but here already. Look for help from this Truth.

August 2, 1891

*The 'little blue magazine' is the Christian Science magazine, first published in 1888 and nicknamed the Little Blue Book for its blue cover.

39

Lesson VI

SELF-CONDEMNATION

John 5:17-30

All is Mind and Mind's ideas. Every idea unfurls itself from your mind, as the pattern within a roll of cloth unrolls and exposes itself. Every thought we think first exposes itself in our own body, and then in our circumstances and environments.

The mind is a garden-bed where the thoughts spring up. We are the husbandmen keeping the garden — each one our own garden. Another cannot sow a seed in our garden unless we please. And there is no hiding what thoughts we have chosen to think when the pattern of them unrolls itself and shows our body and acquaintances. If once we let an angry thought arise in the mind we may be sure that there will be a bad state of our blood, and that somebody will get very angry with us, and also that some angry-acting circumstance will surround us. The pattern of our thought which

41

we let spring up within us does not show forth, sometimes, for months or even years.

You see the first statement of this lesson is, *"My Father worketh hitherto, and I work."* This is the Law of mind, to think and show forth. So we think and show forth our thoughts as our Origin, Mind, does. If we once thought an unjust thought we must not be surprised if the physical affliction we suffer seems very unjust when we have tried to be so good. Then there is the man or the woman who uses us so unjustly; then the circumstances and environments seem unjust.

This lesson for today takes up our thought of self-condemnation which we once indulged in, and shows us how to speak words and think thoughts, which will utterly undo the results of our self-condemnation. Jesus Christ voluntarily took upon Himself all our experiences after they have fruited in the worst possible consequences, and made it very plain for us to know exactly what to do.

Sometimes we condemn ourselves for having done exactly what we ought to have done, as if, for instance, it were against the rules of the house where we were stopping, to feed beggars. But we had not only fed one, but taken her in and washed and dressed her because we saw that she was a good, worthy woman. There in Jerusalem, it was against the law of the city to heal a man in public on the Sabbath as Jesus had healed the paralytic man at the pool of Bethesda.

If you will read this (John 5:17-20) you will find out what to do and say when your motive was all right, but things have turned out all wrong because you condemned yourself, and now people are blaming you terribly. You are to let the motive be its own justification. A good motive is the power of God working in you to will and to do of its own good pleasure. Just lean hard on the motive itself and declare as Jesus Christ did: *"God moveth and I must act."*

The Bethesda lesson, which introduces this, is quite important. A man had been paralyzed in body thirty-eight years to show that once he thought a wrong thought. Bethesda means Healing Mercy; nobody ever had even a whole garden bed of sickening thoughts but what he vaguely or definitely thought of mercy at the same time.

Many people have put their thoughts of healing mercy together and caused an angel (which means pure thought, manifest or unmanifest) to come and stir their conscious minds to a quickening faith in actual healing. They saw their thought manifest as a lovely being stirring the pool, and into this they dipped their sick. But this man had thought a thought, which had now externalized in even his environments being paralyzed. Do you see by this how it is that so many people are not cured of their diseases even by the combined healing thoughts of their acquaintances? Do you not see that it takes the presence of Jesus Christ, face to

43

face with all the power of the Jesus Christ word, to heal certain kinds of troubles?

Now, no matter what the garden of your mind, where the thoughts spring up, may be full of, just know this, that you are given power to pull up and burn whatever thoughts you have thought, and if you will close the soil of your mind tightly around one word, not allowing another single word to grow up there till the full ministry of this new word is accomplished, you will find that everything in your experience will be different.

According to this lesson the word we must speak is Jesus Christ. Every word carries its own quality of power with us and through us and by us and for us when we speak it. Notice that no other word of Healing Mercy availed this man at the pool except Jesus Christ. *"In Him is all the fullness of the Godhead bodily."*

The Egyptians, Persians, Greeks and Romans all used to heal by names. They wrought many miracles by giving all their mind to the holding of one name to the exclusion of every other name. But there was always a point where their names stopped its potency. The name always carried the idea of its ministry or the ministry of the man who bore it. As his ministry was limited and imperfect, his name suggested limitation.

Once, *"In the beginning the Word was God"* but by thinking of God as a Being sending pain and trouble, a veil has come over the name to us, and since the unlimited perfect ministry of Jesus

44

Christ we have to speak that name with our whole heart till all the perfect work which His name conveys is manifested in us. "There is none other name given under heaven whereby we can be saved." So there are certain ones among you who will never be healed, never helped out of your troubles, till you have spoken the name, Jesus Christ, with your whole mind as intent upon it as it is possible for it to be. The names David, John, Moses, anybody else but Jesus, carry a panorama of limitation, failure, sin.

The faith-cure people have wrought many miracles in the name of Jesus, but it is noticeable how afraid they are of draughts, night airs, accidents, other religious beliefs, etc. So there is not perfect ministry by them. The Christian Scientists have wrought many miracles by the name of Christ, carefully explained as Truth, but there have been divisions, strifes, intolerance among them and thus there has been something lacking. So now this lesson explains, that is the verses before the seventeenth do, that it must be by the whole name that we are to be wholly saved.

When the officers asked of Peter and John in whose name they healed the man born lame, they answered, "In the name of Jesus Christ." Do not stop to explain the word. Make haste to clear your mind of its old errors, exactly as the lesson of July twenty-sixth declares, and proceed to hold the full word Jesus Christ till the full ministry is done in you and you have clear access to the Father. This makes you equal with Jesus Christ in the power of the Spirit, as He promised.

"Where I Am there ye may be also" "Ask in my name."

Jesus Christ, on this occasion, while showing us what to do when we seem to have broken some man-made law, taught us that as He troubled the old Jewish Sabbath right near the place where the angel troubled the waters, so we may put all actions prompted by high notices onto the responsibility of The Father or The Spirit which is the good motive itself, and need not explain ourselves.

Only *"What He seeth the Father do."* The Father is Love. Only what Love bids us do can we do if we have a good motive. Good Motive is God. God is Love. *"Sheweth Him all things."* We are shown exactly what to do under all circumstances and in all places. The son of God is the perfect motive to do good. *"The Son quickeneth whom He will."* The perfect word in the mind will quicken those who seem dead. We shall see the whole name Jesus Christ quicken the dullest and stupidest people to thinking so harmoniously that the red blood will flow swiftly, the hard joints will limber, and the eyes will flash with light. This name spoken will teach us to raise the quickening life and beauty of our friends into plain sight.

"He that believeth shall not come into condemnation." This text is the main point for self-treatment when all things point to our having

made some seemingly very false moves which nobody approves. We must deny self-condemnation and the condemnation of others. "There is no condemnation." Do not forget to say, "I am not under self-condemnation. I am not under the law of condemnation." Your mind will clear itself, and you can speak the word Jesus Christ unto swift power.

"The resurrection of life and the resurrection of damnation" said Jesus. He meant that you would see the life of the True Word demonstrated and the death or disappearance of the false word. The idea of condemnation of good motives for any actions, the idea of persecution for the Jesus Christ healing, will be demonstrated as pure nothingness.

"My judgment is just." Why is the Jesus Christ judgment just? Because no earthly ambition is consulted. The Jesus Christ word makes you no time-server. You are on the side of Omnipotence when you are in the right. Lean hard on the right and say, as Jesus did, *"All power is given unto Me because My judgment is just."* When Abraham Lincoln was asked if he was sure God was on His side, he answered, "I am not so much concerned to know whether God is on my side as whether I am on God's side."

"Be strong, and of a good courage; fear not nor be afraid of them; for the Lord thy God, He it is that doth go with thee; He will not fail thee, nor forsake thee."

August 9, 1891

47

Lesson VII

FEEDING THE STARVING

John 6:1-14

This lesson is about Jesus Christ's going across the Sea of Galilee, up into a mountain and sitting down to the working out of a problem of human life.

The going across the sea, instead of around it, is a hint of the metaphysical Law of taking the straight line as the shortest distance between two points. By this lesson I know that there is no need of waiting for summer and winter, seed time and harvest to feed people. Also, Jesus Christ settled the question for all time as to the duty of the spiritual or Christian teacher in the matter of feeding the multitudes as well as healing and comforting them.

You may be sure that there is a short cut or direct route to all accomplishments. French and music should be learned at once without long years of drill. Success is your immediate right without years of painstaking effort. Are you not one with the Origin of all power and all knowledge? Does that substance or divine region of you have to learn anything? No. Let the Divine of you reign and, like Jesus Christ, you enter at once upon your inheritance.

Simply because you have heretofore gone around and not across the sea of your life, need not count against your acceptance of the divine guidance now with you and for you and in you. Jesus of Nazareth settled the question once of what to do when falsely condemned; of what to do when deserted by your friends and in humiliation; of what to do when there is a death in your family; of what to do with sickness; of what to do when you yourself are buried in a tomb past all hope.

Today He settles the question of feeding starving people. This vital spark of divinity you now represent might be fanned by you into a living, quickening fire of bright genius if you would let it have its way. Genius always does things in a new, unexpected way. Napoleon conquered armies, not by the usual arts of war or military tactics, but in his own way. Abe Lincoln won victories and ran the government to a new tune. Jesus Christ took this time to set aside the circuit of summer and winter and seed time and harvest and make bread at once. He explained the modus operandi of quick accomplishments. Elijah once kept a widow's cruse full at Zarephath. Elisha replenished one at Gilgal and fed one hundred men with twenty loaves of bread, but neither of them explained the process. Jesus here explains it.

First. *"He went up into a mountain and sat down."* This means that He went into an exalted state of mind. There is no power of healing in a depressed state of mind. There is no quickening of the exhausted by a sorrowful or anxious state of mind. In order to work your best, metaphysically, you must be in an exalted state of mind. Now, there are two ways of getting into an exalted state of mind: there is the short and direct way of Jesus and there is the longer but just as sure way of Job.

The short, direct way of Jesus Christ is the one now used by the Christian scientists. It is by denial and affirmation, as explained three or four weeks ago. You remember that He denied the reality of material things by saying, *"The flesh profiteth nothing"* He denied the power of evil by saying, *"It is a lie from the beginning."* He affirmed, *"All power is given unto Me"* and *"I and the Father are one."* His manner of speaking has a very exalting effect upon the mind, and to rest in that state of exaltation is the sure healing of your sick mother and the sure bringing to pass of success. Exaltation is a magnet for all good things of the universe to hasten to you. Depression and anxiety are a magnet for trouble to fly to you.

But you are saying, "How can I be other than depressed and anxious when my father has failed in business, my brother is a drunkard, and my mother is paralyzed?" Then you must take Job's

51

way of getting into an exalted state of mind. Job reasoned with the Almighty. He told the Almighty face to face that His own hands having fashioned him he could not be wicked and that he would maintain his righteous cause before Him.

This reasoning out your own case with that divine Presence that folds you so close is a mighty help to your state of mind, and never was known to fail anybody.

The great account made of "sparrows" fills our hearts with gladness. A man who had to feed the solders in a camp, was ordered to give them half slices at a time when they had been extra worked and were extra hungry. He reasoned with the divine Goodness as a man talketh with his brother, that according to the righteous law of supply and demand, these men should have double rations instead of half ones. Then he ordered his under officer to double the thickness of the slices, and before he got through distributing the first lot a wagon load of provisions drove into camp.

Be sure to be very definite in stating your case. Do not let your emotion consume your words. Be on hand to mumble out something besides intense emotion of grief, or anger, or fear. The "Word" is very essential. *"Without the Word was nothing made" "If a man eat of the Word I give him, though he were dead, yet shall he live again."*

Then when your mind gets into an exalted state, trust God. "Whom have I in heaven but Thee, and there is none upon earth that I desire beside Thee." This is the confidence of mind which Jesus emphasized by sitting down in the mountain. Now, in this calm state of confidence, you may take deliberate account of your assets and liabilities.

The same is true in cases of illness and domestic sorrow, as in this case of penury or seeming failure of supplies in running your home or affairs of any kind. So if we understand this case, we understand all cases. You take account of liabilities and necessities. That is your Philip thought. Notice how Philip said that there were five thousand people and it would take thirty-four dollars worth of bread to feed them. Andrew told the assets, *"Five barley loaves and two fishes."* Without noticing the hopeless calculations of Philip or the tiny comfort of Andrew, Jesus Christ bade the five thousand to "sit down on the grass" just exactly as if there were plenty on hand.

So you, when your faith hath come into its word, "All my trust on Thee is staid; all my health from Thee I bring," do you go right on with your affairs and works just exactly as if your bounty was visible. This is not the time to economize and withhold. This is the time to use right up to the last of the assets, right on to the heels of the last penny, as the two widows poured freely forth what seemed the last of the meal and the oil.

Every stroke you make towards penuriousness and retrenchment of fair expenses will cost you double. This is the time when you look up and give thanks for your assets, give loving thanks for five loaves and two fishes to do a five-thousand-dollar business with.

Jesus Christ did not roam around despising the meeting of people on their own ground of wants, but He found out their wants and wills and met them there. Who cares about flying around a throne on wings with our children and mothers after death, when a good home and ability to make it happy here is what the heart craves.

Jesus Christ helped people here to see that there is in themselves all power to get out of every condition undesirable and, beyond that, the ability to do great works in proof of Sonship and Oneness with the One who created them. Nothing is too small or too simple to reason with Jesus Christ about. Jesus Christ is God manifest. To reason with Him is to become more and more merged in Him.

By this time you have caught the secret of reasoning with Jesus Christ, or the Almighty. You cannot help seeing that if we become like those we converse with we should soon become so lost in the knowledge of the Character of Jesus Christ that His very miracle-working power would be ours. You have now caught the Principle, have you not, that if you describe God you become exactly as great as you describe God to be, as fast as you realize what you are talking?

So if you praise God as Supreme giving— Supreme bounty—you may hand out and hand out

and hand out, for back of you is infinite supply.
"There is that scattereth and yet increaseth, and
there is that withholdeth more that is meet and
tendeth to poverty."

This teaches that God is unto us according to
our faith; therefore dreadfully economical people
do not have much faith if they carry their careful
saving unto hoarding up lest they come to want. If
they hoard for giving farther after all the present
bounty has filled their neighbors, they will increase it and increase it till they have to call to the
streets of foreign cities to get people enough to
partake of their bountiful stores. Wonderful words
are those with which you describe the Almighty.
They react on you so wonderfully. They are alive.
There is no wonder that so many people have said,
"There is no God only the one you imagine, because you get exactly what you imagine God to be
giving."

Then again, it was a very good expression of
one man to say, "An honest God is the noblest
work of man," because if you describe God as revengeful you soon get revengeful; if you describe
God as love and justice you soon become just and
loving. If you describe God as niggardly and apt to
send afflictions you soon get stingy and full of sorrows.

This lesson enjoins strict reasoning, strict
truth—right description of God.

August 16, 1891

55

Lesson VIII

THE BREAD OF LIFE

John 6:26-40

It is one of the first teachings of metaphysics that all environments, circumstances, conditions, all the people who come near us, and everything else, existed first as ideas in our own mind and now appear in plain sight to be known and read plainly.

The science of metaphysics, which Jesus Christ taught deals with the meta, beyond, and physics, i.e., that is beyond, out of the range of, the physical. The mental is the metaphysical.

This being true, he is our greatest teacher who can tell us how to think such thoughts as shall keep us from making failures, sorrows, blind people, deaf people, inferior people, hard circumstances to surround us. He is our greatest teacher who can tell us how to make harmonious circumstances, success in our undertakings, perfect people to surround us. He is our greatest teacher who can tell us how to redeem our life from those failures, hardships, poor people, our former thoughts have fruited into.

He will be our divinely good friend who shall teach us to think such thoughts as shall cause us to sit down in due season under the vine and fig-tree of our exactly right ideas.

Jesus Christ is this teacher and this friend. There was no circumstance and no condition, which we have walled ourselves into that He did not take upon Himself and teach us how to redeem ourselves from the consequences of our erring thoughts. Redemption was the story Jesus Christ taught. And redemption is the theme of all these lessons, where He is making an object lesson of Himself for our benefit.

He taught us to say, *"How I am glorified,"* when physical anguish and desertion of friends come upon us for believing in the power of evil and the reality of matter. Have you learned the lesson so well that you also have redeemed yourself from physical anguish and have chosen unto yourself many loving friends when you seem to have none? No? Then you need not be surprised if anguish still gets a hold on you and you still feel lonely. Words are ideas. True words are alive and good.

So if you are in the deeps of sorrow, you speak living words that can bear your mind out on their wings into a paradise of peace.

"True words are angels.

What matter smile or frown.

If angels looking down,

Do each to other talk of thee

In tones of love continually,

Until thy name on earth seldom heard Hath

come to be in heaven a household word."

Once a woman believed that Jesus Christ meant it as a signal to her of what to say for her feet, which had a habit of paining excruciatingly. So she said: *"Father, how Thou has glorified me."* And she felt as if she were actually being borne upon wings of delight, so free and at peace her feet hastened to be.

He taught us what to say when we have come to our last dollar and have no visible means of support. He taught us what to say when we are condemned by our family and neighbors for having acted according to our highest light. He here condescends to our low estate where we have brought around us a tribe of sycophants, or people who think of us as simply a provider, and feeder, and caretaker for them.

He here shows us what state of mind we must have been in to have caused such a state of affairs. He shows that it has been because of our mixed beliefs, as first we have believed in the necessity for hard work to accomplish that which we wished to accomplish; and secondly, we have been ambitious for fame of some kind, some earthly honor or emolument; thirdly, we have believed that we ought to carry out our own will at whatever cost somewhere or sometime along our journey over this planet.

The people who followed Jesus this time went for the food, not for His doctrine at all. He takes us at the point where we realize that people want to use us, not to honor us by being near us. You have all had this experience more or less, and it always stands for the coming to outward expression of your self-will, ambition, and belief in the great results of hard work.

The Christian scientist often has this state of affairs, and is grieved by it. He or she has the definite instruction of what to do with the thoughts to be "raised up" at the last extremity of such a situation. Perhaps it might all be summed up in that general statement of Truth, which the scientist makes when learning the lessons of mental responsibility. "There is no life, substance, or intelligence in matter;" but this direction is much more explicit than that, and tells you to deny that there is any necessity in your lot for hard labor, deny that you ever hoped great things from earthy honors, and deny emphatically that you were ever self-willed.

When the Christian scientist suddenly discovers that her patient is not her friend and does not believe in the science, though he has said he was and did, but was only making believe in order to get his arms cured, failing which, for a time he repudiates the whole doctrine and his obligations of every kind to her, she is grieved and astonished, often discouraged.

Now, nobody has any more religion than just as much as he can command in time of trial. This religion of Jesus teaches you exactly what to do and say to redeem yourself from grief, disappointment, failure. Also that if you deal exactly right with your own mind, the people around you will spring right up into right conditions. Even the patient who shows that he or she just looked upon you as a useful penwiper or doormat for them and so were not promptly cured, he will be cured if you understand this lesson. Jesus Christ did not despise healing the people, feeding them, furnishing money or anything else for them. He did not look down upon any humble ministry, but He knew that to look at money for its own sake, or feed for its own sake, or healing for its own sake, is a belief in the value of earthly things, which must be denied. There must be no belief in the necessity for hard labor in anybody's lot. Rest remaineth for the people of God as to manual labor for meat, bread, house, health.

The seeking of God first through faithfully speaking right words will bring anybody into such spiritual power that "all these things are added" without effort. Ambition to merit reward by works is discountenanced by Jesus Christ. Nobody is saved by works. Salvation by works was the early teaching of Christian science as set forth by William S. Adams fifty years ago in his book on Christian science. John Knox was told that his good works would save him. He fought all night against the belief that they would. He came into the understanding that faith in Jesus Christ, or believing the Word of Christ, which is Truth, was salvation.

Here Jesus Christ urges every man, woman, and child to believe in the heart what is true, and this believing, or right faith, will feed, clothe, support them. This one must do by words that are right, very vigorously uttered, when he has been brought up to believe that his bread and butter for himself and family are dependent upon his hard efforts. It is a bad idea to get its hold in any mind. Ben Franklin had that belief so hard that he ran it into a saving-up and hoarding state of mind that nearly warped the happiness out of the lot of nearly all the farmers' children of New England.

It is a very unspiritual idea, and must be boldly handled, torn up by the roots, out of mind. Say positively: "I do not believe in hard work as necessary for myself or anybody else to live comfortably in God's universe." This saving by works will make a man or woman who has struggled hard, feel that he or she has earned some rights to extra blessings in heaven. It will cause a certain class of mind to think that outward actions will satisfy all the demands of God on the soul, as Admiral Nelson, who broke his wife's heart, but did so much service to his country, felt sure he had earned the right to an extra good place in heaven.

The Lord looketh on the heart! Nothing is worth working for except a right state of mind. All the greatest, good men and women the world has ever known have found out a great principle of life in the knowledge that we are not walking over this planet for the purpose of making for ourselves a great name, gathering to ourselves riches, honors, friends, but to do the will of God in that estate whereunto we are called.

The preacher must come to where he knows it is not to convert men to Christ not to make the world better, not to be great in the cause of God, but to do the will of God willingly. The will of God often pushes the great man or the great woman into the quick fruits of his mistaken thoughts, so that he is in mean and small circumstances, out of which he must extricate himself by speaking the same simple truths the wash-woman and hod-carrier must speak. He will find himself in great extremities, or "at the last day," as Jesus here in this lesson expresses it. But if he do the will of God, or meekly speak the right words he will be "raised up."

The righteous man often has a belief in hard labor, is ambitious to be great, is self-willed, so he has great things depending upon his efforts, has people depending upon him who ought to be doing for themselves, and is harassed by the failures of his plans or their delay in coming out right till he is brought to great extremities. He must take the denial of Jesus, "I came not to do mine own will. I do not care for earthly honors. I am no time server."

Then when he has said in all sincerity, "I am doing the will of God," this denial and affirmation will cause his plans to be "raised up". They will be wonderfully successful. He himself will be honored. He will be "raised up" in joy and delight. Notice that the "raised up" is, first, for the works or plans, and second for the man. All things were taught by this man of God, Jesus Christ. He is our highest idea of man as a Son of God. If you understand Him, you will be redeemed from and will redeem your world from evil.

August 23, 1891

Lesson IX

THE CHIEF THOUGHT

John 7:31-34

"When Christ Cometh," These people were expecting a Messiah or Christ. That which they were expecting as a body of people, each one of us is always expecting.

Look carefully into your own mind, examine your kingdom of thoughts, and you will see that there is always a region of you which is intensely looking for deliverance from your environments. This is your Jewry. Now your Christ or deliverer is standing right in yourself, telling you the exact way out this minute.

Job said: *"Is not my help in me?"* Within me is one thought, that if I heed it will lift me out of every situation and circumstance which the Roman yoke on the Jews typified. So with you. What is true of you is true of every sentient thing. Now the Christ thought in you, which will save you, you do not let have its way with you. Why don't you?

65

Each mind is a kingdom of thoughts. We have all power over the kingdom of our own thoughts. We may let a Pharisaic thought or a chief priest thought shut off the beautiful one within us, which always says "I Am thy Savior."

Hush all your realm of thoughts for a moment and let that one which says "I am Christ" speak. You can actually work miracles if you let that thought have full sway over your other thoughts. These lessons of Jesus Christ among the Jews and Gentiles represent your Jesus Christ thought within yourself. Each thought says, "I am." You let that one have reign over you which you please. "I am envy," says one thought; "I am bigotry," says another; "I am success," says another; "I am your savior from all evil," says the greatest One within your realm.

This greatest thought is your oldest thought. It was with you in the beginning, is with you now, and ever shall be with you, world without end. It is the "Ancient of Days," "Come and reign over us, Ancient of Days."

Notice this, if you please, that your pious thought, representing the traditions of the past as to the severity of God, is quick to take and bind your Jesus Christ thought. Your Pharisaic thought, representing your past teachings as to your inferiority before God, always chokes down the generous, Sabbath-breaking Christ thought.

Now Jesus Christ, or the power of Truth, is in you all. This power of Truth you cannot kill, but you may hide it if you please for a while, "Yet a little while am I with you," it says just as quickly as your piety and bigotry are roused. For the power of God is never manifested where pious bigotry is allowed rule.

When this knowledge of the ways of thoughts in the mind became known to some very brave thinkers they voluntarily let all their thoughts keep perfect silence while the Jesus Christ thought spoke in them, saying; "I Am the Messiah. I Am Jesus Christ." They all reported wonderful experiences. It seemed to them as if their whole being was God being. There was nothing but God "above them all and through them all and in them all." Jesus Christ is God. This is not person, but Principle, Jesus Christ is the voice, the power of God. These people all became strong through and through. They became well and sound through and through.

Their judgment became strong and healthy. They are sure that if you will not let your old prejudices blind you, but will let your highest thought have freedom, you will rise like a bird out of the snare of the fowler, free in God.

Listen to that highest idea within your realm of ideas. Here is its message: *"If any man thirst, let him come unto Me, and drink."* You know you are thirsty for something. If your friends love you, you still are thirsty. If you have money you still are thirsty. If you have fame you still are thirsty. If you are learned in books you still are thirsty. You will always be thirsty for something till you let your highest idea reign over you.

It says: "I am your lover, your friend, your counselor, your satisfaction." There is no other way of receiving Jesus Christ except this one. It is the principle that is never absent from the mind of any man or woman or child. No matter what you have done or thought, if you will let your thoughts all hold still for this one to rise in its majesty, you are good and great and wise and healthy that moment. The satisfaction of living is yours when forth from you flows the living water of your highest idea only. This is not the doctrine of salvation by works. It is not the doctrine of salvation by faith in anybody or anything.

It is salvation by the "let there be" of Moses and Jesus of Nazareth. It was by keeping silent for God to be the whole of Him that Jesus was enabled to say so boldly, *"I and the Father are one. He that hath seen Me hath seen the Father."* Spinoza was so lost in finding the power of God over and through and in him so wonderfully, that he was called the God-intoxicated man.

Many people have been afraid to let their Jesus Christ thought be their only thought. It seemed suddenly to them as if they themselves were all Jesus Christ, all God, nothing else of them. Why they could possibly be afraid to have their mind occupied by one perfect idea is a mystery. To hold back from speaking this idea in the mind, or rather letting the idea speak itself, is to put off the power of the Holy Ghost (according to this lesson).

The Holy Ghost is the quickening power of God. The Holy Ghost has not come while you are sick, while you are poor, while you are lame, while you are unhappy. And you cannot have the Holy Ghost till you have been silent enough for the Jesus Christ idea that is within your realm of ideas to speak its words within you very definitely.

Do not be afraid of being Jesus Christ. Do not be afraid of any experience that comes with letting this wonderful idea speak within you. Do not let your thoughts rise up with all kind of babblings like they did in the Nazareth Man's time. They said, *"Shall Christ come out of Galilee?"*

You may comfort yourself by knowing that the high doctrine of "Let these be" says, *"Let the same mind be in you that was in Christ Jesus our Lord."* Your mind is not too low a place for your best thoughts to reign over your poor ones in. The poor ones are completely redeemed when they lie still as death for that ever present one to say, "I Am thy Messiah. I Am thy Savior, thy Friend, thy Counselor, thy mighty Judgment, thy Power and Majesty forever."

Here the Jews refused the Messiah because they feared that Galilee was not good enough for Him to come out of. You are exactly that when you think you are not good enough to have a thought anywhere within you, which is the Savior, the Righteous.

69

Some men have not let this thought in their mind be Jesus Christ. Because that word seemed to them to be a man with a religious system to urge and not a principle, so they have let this supreme thought within them say, "I am God, and I reign over thee." Now, in the beginning that was indeed the Word, but by accusing God of so many dealings He could not possibly be guilty of, we have all drawn a veil over our faces, and the Deep crying unto Deep within us saying, "I am God," does not bring the power of God so quickly as by letting the idea Jesus Christ be spoken till the veil is rent. At the same time there is no difference in the meaning of the words. The principle idea within your mind is the God idea. You are expected to work miracles. Every one of you who takes this mode of dealing with the mind will find yourselves converted to uprightness, rejoiced with new powers, filled with health. There is nothing out of the power of one who lets all his mind rest for one thought only to speak. You have the power to call back those who are called dead. You have the power to turn copper into gold. There are strange powers lying dormant, as it were, within you, which keeping all your thoughts still for one thought to rise in its glory, would quicken. This is the "mystery of Godliness." It is spoken of as the Lion of David, because only victorious people are supposed to have the powers of God with them. But everybody is a victory over the world by this process. There is nothing to do, nothing to believe, only "Let be what is; let speak what is true."

70

Of course you have heard that Truth is Omnipotence. I assure you that it is. Let speak within you that secret, silent word, while all your other thoughts lie low. "Behold, I have put My Name upon thee." Even while you thirst for the child to be well, the home to be harmonious, the environments not to cramp you so, behold in your midst, that is, in your realm of thoughts, stands the Christ.

So now you see how the kingdom of Heaven is within you. Many people are letting this thought in the midst of them speak till there is great meekness and lowliness of heart where before was pride and arrogance. They do not care for name and fame and rule where before they were ambitious. Your highest thought is meek and lowly of heart.

Let the night watches find you still while your highest "I am" speaks. All that you dream of as desirable is in that redeeming word. So many people catching this knowledge of the metaphysical instructions given by Jesus Christ for our example are the hastening on of that time of which the prophet spoke, *"Many saviors shall come up from Jerusalem."* Jerusalem means peace. So from the peace of letting thoughts lie still for the Christ one to say, "I Am thy Redeemer," saviors are springing up all over the earth. "They shall all be taught of God" is the prophecy. This God-thought that waits within you, being let to say, "I am" will teach you all things and remind you of that country from whence you came forth and unto which you return.

71

You have a wonderful kingdom of thoughts. Which one reigns now?

August 30, 1891

Lesson X

CONTINUE THE WORK

John 8:31-47

"If ye continue in My Word," said Jesus Christ, *"then are ye my disciples."* This discourse of Jesus before the Jews in the court of the Temple at Jerusalem is all about the Power of the Word.

If anyone is unaware of the potency of the idea he is holding in mind to strike out over his daily affairs and into his bodily conditions then he is not yet acquainted with Christian doctrine.

Take the idea that you are at this moment holding. What is it? The strongest idea one set of people hold is that if something does not turn up within a certain time only a miracle can save them from something or other that is threatening. This is an idea that makes the atmosphere strained and attenuated and gives the children nervous cramps, and the rest of the family neuralgia.

73

Take that idea and change it into this one: "I have a right to the best, and I will trust to my rights to bring me out right."

As your child has a right to your love and to your protection, and trusts his right, so have you a right to protection in this universe into which you are born.

Trust bravely. Trust like a child and a potentate. Socrates said that a state of grief or anxiety would attract sickness, waste of property, and death. Grief is a word held in the mind. A word is an idea.

"For the lightest word thou shall give account." The words of Jesus Christ, He promised, would lead into comfort, joy, peace, power. Alike attracts like. You hold a strong, loving thought on purpose; hold it tenaciously; directly, strong loving successes will crown your efforts. This is metaphysics. This is a psychologic study left out in the school books, but is, indeed, the metaphysics of Jesus Christ.

Here He shows what will be the effect of speaking His words, which are all true. Ye shall be free. *"The Truth shall make you free."*

The Truth He told is so stupendous that many a noble preacher has refused to speak it. Take this word He told you to speak, for instance, "I and the Father are one." People think mostly that He meant only Jesus of Nazareth was one with God.

Not at all. He meant that you and I are one with the Father, *"Where I Am there ye may be also."*

You are looking for freedom of some sort. The fact that you are searching for freedom is evidence that you do not know Truth. "The Truth makes free," remember.

The Russian peasant cowered and shrank like a frightened spaniel while he believed that the shadows in the field were filled with vampires, but when he knew that there was no such thing as a vampire in the shadow he stood up and walked free. The Truth made him free. When you know that a draught of air has no neuralgia or rheumatism in it for you, you will not shrink and cower like a spaniel when a damp draught strikes you. "The truth shall make you free."

"But," you say, "the damp draught does give me neuralgia." No. That idea of yours about the failure of your business, or the injustice of your neighbor, or the envious thought against another, brought the neuralgia. "Oh but." You say, "my little innocent child has the neuralgia from the damp air." No, it has not; it was your idea that folded it around like a magnet to draw trouble unto its little self. "Envy is the rottenness of the bones," says the Scripture.

To believe in the claims of weather, inheritance, climate, etc., is to be in bondage. There is a way of getting free from the effects of false words in good science. You take each word as it comes into your mind and mix it and mold it and rectify it by right words till you would never know it to be the word you set out with.

Each word of Truth is a setting-free principle. The Scriptures are true. See how senile decrepitude is getting the bondage over your eyesight. Do you know that instead of losing your sight as the years go on you ought to increase in sight? Can you imagine what idea made you put on glasses? It was something along the line of your human experience which you said about the "Lord having dealt very bitterly by you," or making your lot hard, or your burden heavy.

This compels you to take up that thought which, though it lies unconscious in your realm is there just the same, and needs rectifying. Say to the old past, bitter cry, "I see that God is good to me, God is good to me." Mold and mold that old-time word till it raises within you a joyous certainty that God is indeed good to you. Then your eyesight will return to you.

Suppose that your hearing is feeble. That shows that you have had many gods or idol. Some things have been very, very dear to you, or very, very powerful over you. "Hear, O Israel, the Lord our God is One." Take your dearest treasure or your greatest fear and say, "There is only One God — One." Soon your hearing will be restored. In this lesson Jesus Christ speaks of continuing in His Word. By this He intimates what deaf and blind often do, begin good words and drop speaking them soon. "Repetition is the mother of wisdom." If you keep speaking the right word, which is the word that fits your particular case, you will get great light on the principle involved by the word. This is explained by the speed with which a child understands the principle of the multiplication table, if he speaks it much.

There are reasons why sight and hearing must be mentioned in this connection, it seems; notice how He speaks of what He sees with His father and what they see and do with their father. Sight and hearing are entirely dependent upon our own ideas of God. Wrong ideas of God are now causing the whole human race to show out deafness and blindness as never before. Even the children are getting blind and deaf. "The earth waxeth old as a garment." Those of us who changed radically our ideas of God began to have very acute hearing and wonderful clearness of vision far superior to the eyesight and hearing of our childhood. Then there began to be quickened another visual and another auditory power besides the regular.

"Awake, O earth!" "Arise, shine, for thy light is come." "Awake! Arise!" "Rise from the dead, and Christ shall give thee light."

There are some new ideas going about the decrepit eye that everybody carries in his head; not an embryonic or crude eye, but an aged eye; aged as our other two eyes are getting to be in the race head. The true doctrine renews the strength of the aged; try the true doctrine. The true doctrine renews the vigor and vitality of those who are stepping over the lines into weakness; try the true doctrine. The new doctrine quickens that other seeing and hearing faculty within the already young and vigorous till they can see that other dimension in space which Jesus Christ saw so plainly.

There are said to be people who can untie knots, which the most skillful cannot loosen, because by an unexplainable faculty they can do it. They use without knowing it, the fourth dimension in space. This quickened seeing faculty enables one to sit down and scan his own universe and set it into such order as he wishes it. You know, do you not, that any tangle in your affairs is the sign of incomplete knowledge? The true knowledge would untie the knot. There is one little link, one little point which would set everything right in a moment.

So lovely and practical is the teaching of Jesus Christ that you cannot possibly miss knowing exactly what to do under all circumstances if you follow His directions. Do not be too proud to sit meekly down at His feet and learn about the fourth dimension in space. Learn the quickening words of our Father which He told us. He calls the word of Truth "the Son." He urges us all to get free by the Son, or the word continually spoken. He was aware that if your hearing and sight are quickened by "the Son" or "the Word", there will be no going back. Mechanical appliances and material compounds are sure to lose their powers. So do

the words of the strong human will or the mes-
meric touch; but "if the Son make you free, ye are
free indeed." He brings up Abraham to show that
mere belief in physical descent is no healing or
setting-free principle.

It must be the quickening word of "the Son" in
them, just as it was in Abraham, by which they
shall be free. Unless they had that they were only
children of the devil, or error, and would have the
senile ear and eye, and tangle in affairs forever.
Abraham was quickened by trusting in God su-
premely as the Only Spirit. Abraham called every
dream and every vision he had "a word of the
Lord," till he got so he was complete master over
all things. While people were wondering, halting,
doubting, Abraham was trusting God.

These Jews knew nothing of such faith, and
were therefore nowhere near being children of
Faith. Just know that every single affair lies
clearly soluble by a right word in the mind. Walk
close to God with the words, *"I and the Father are
One, I tell you the Truth."* Notice that the golden
text of this lesson is the gist of it all, *"As many as
received Him, to them gave He power to become the
sons of God."* To receive Christ is to become the
Christ through and through. The Christ is the Son
of God. The Son of God has all power, has all
knowledge. As you are well aware that you are
children of God already, you know that this "be-
coming" simply means that you show forth your
powers.

79

There is nothing will pay you like the continual repetition of the words of Jesus Christ. You will soon be quickened through and through. There is the very power of God within you folded as a rosebud folds its petals and sepals and perfumes. His words will cause you to show forth your powers. What do you claim that you are? A little feeble child? Then you are drooping round with very limited powers. Do you claim to be a poor worm of the dust? Then you are prematurely old. Do you claim to be inferior in your nature to Jesus Christ? Then you are still wondering when the world will grow to love each other and do right by each other. Are you claiming that environments make you? Then you are an idolater, and subject to contagious and increasing liabilities to disease.

Why don't you spring forth the potentiality of that nature with which you were vested before the days of Abraham? In other words, why don't you say: "I and the Father are One;" "All power is given unto me;" "I arise from my dream of error, I know my royal descent and my universal privileges, by my noblest word let me be judged."

This will cause you to make the atonement manifest. This will manifest your unity with the Christ. Unity with the Christ is marriage with the Holy Spirit. Union with the Holy Spirit is atonement. I will speak to you about the atonement next time.

Meanwhile, quicken your powers — resurrect them into the sight of all the world by

80

understanding this lesson as treating of your absolute freedom and absolute power in Spirit, and your nothingness and powerlessness as materiality.

"This is the judgment in its birth;

Tis thus our Lord approaches earth.

Rise on thy noblest word.

Rest thou one with Christ the Lord."

Defy death. Defy pain. Defy weakness. Quicken — quicken into satisfactory living by true words.

September 6, 1891

Lesson XI

INHERITANCE OF SIN

John 9:1-11, 35-38

This lesson of Christ and the blind man includes the whole Christian doctrine of salvation. It takes in the Christian teachings of all the Christians before the time of Jesus and since His time. Christ means truth; so all truth speaking is Christian teaching. Here in this lesson is the whole scheme of salvation by works, faith, and atonement. The pious Dervish and the modern churchman are trying to get into heaven by appeasing their deity with "works." But there is nothing heavenly about the lot or looks of either of these types of workers for salvation. It is only one side of the triangle of religious law. Incompleteness is always unsatisfactory.

The trial at salvation from evil, by the practice of the mind called faith is also unsatisfactory as heretofore demonstrated. It is only another side of the triangle and is not complete doctrine. Jesus Christ preached "works," as, *"If I do not the works of the Father believe Me not." "Have faith in God." "Have the faith of God."* But He lived and demonstrated atonement or the unity of His mind with the Mind that is God. *"I and the Father are One."*

The effects of the practice of faith are remarkable, almost attracting one to study to have faith. There are two kinds of faith practiced, active and passive. An earnest young man gave all his fortune to the support of the poor, believing that his unseen God would provide for him. He charged nothing for arduous labors, verily believing in a sure sustenance, which, with all that belongs to human necessities, was actually provided always after intense assurances before his unseen God his unshakable faith. A woman who had no faith but had been told what wonder might be wrought through faith sat down and deliberately determined to learn it. She sat down in the midst of her poverty and loneliness with her little children about her and practiced learning. She seemed shiftless to her neighbors, but it was astonishing what "luck" that woman always had. Something good was always "turning up." Her children were all talented, beautiful, prosperous.

Yet there was something lacking. Incompleteness is unsatisfactory. Neither the man or woman type pleased their neighbors by its demonstration well enough to practice it. Faith is a state of mind dependent on the will. Works may be quite external. Faith is mental. Atonement is the understanding and experience of the actual Oneness of the Spirit that is God; of the mind of man with the Mind that is God.

This lesson teaches the whole doctrine of salvation according to Jesus Christ, as to his own duty and experience and the effect of such doctrine in toto upon all who receive it. He took a man "born blind" and healed him. Such blindness was considered incurable then as now by material methods. His disciples ask Him, "Who hath sinned, this man or his parents?" What made them put the man before his parents in the matter of responsibility for that blindness? Why that was the much-talked-of doctrine of reincarnation, whereby a man was not considered new at the time of birth in the flesh, but old from having lived some previous existence and who now deliberately chose certain people for his parents to demonstrate prolonged existence by an experience with earth life.

Jesus Christ promptly denied the whole theory, "Neither hath this man sinned." Whatever of eternal life the man as a sinless spiritual being might have realized, mortal ways were desired and the reincarnation of sin rejected.

In Christian science we always recognize humanity as spiritual and deny the claim of sin in the individual and his ancestors just as Jesus Christ did. We do not believe in an inheritance of sin, *"Neither hath this man sinned, nor his parents."* We believe in an inheritance from God alone. "Hath not His hand fashioned me?" "Thou knowest that I am not wicked." *"Call no man upon earth your Father."*

As it makes a mighty difference to our health what we believe, of course you can see that it is much better to believe that God is our Father than that any other being could hand us down an inheritance. It was a common belief in those days, as now; that we have what we have of disease and pain as a consequence of sin.

But Jesus Christ, who told us to be sure and keep His words and be in a state of mind exactly like His, said, *"Of all that Thou hast given Me, I have lost none save the son of perdition."* "Son" means idea, speaking metaphysically, and since "the flesh profiteth nothing" we will not speak any other way. So "son of perdition" means idea of sin and its history. I drop no idea except the idea of sin — that I reject — for in a universe created by the Good, governed by the Good, occupied by the Good, and tolerating only the Good, there is no reality in sin, so there is no place for sin.

It will cause an appearance of blindness and deafness to hold the idea that there is any reality in evil of any kind. It is a limitation of powers and faculties. *"I set before you an open door."* There is universal freedom with ideas of universal Good.

To keep the mind fixed to a prejudice has a limited effect upon some function of the body. This lesson is about dropping limitations and receiving light. Our missionaries to foreign lands ought to take their mind from looking at the natives through the idea that they are all to be damned if they don't know the history of the man Jesus of Nazareth. That idea has hidden the sight of their eyes and their children's eyes. They do not destroy the sight, but they hide it by an idea.

Milton hid his eyesight by thinking the false idea that there was a Satan in Paradise. We hide our vision by trying to put limitations on our fellow men.

We see a man who says things to God in a laughing, hilarious fashion and we immediately think he ought to be hushed up, but how do we know but that he is a demonstration of the text, "The Lord laugheth in the heavens?" Man can do only one thing for his neighbor — give him his freedom. To throw around you an atmosphere of freedom will make them good — rather, give them a chance to show forth their inherent goodness. Keep hold of this idea of the righteousness of freedom and you will find other faculties of sight and hearing opening up. I do not mean intuition; I mean a present sight as definite as your sight of that book mark and the page you wish to place it in. You have the hidden faculty of seeing what that missing link is, which, if you will look at it, will set your affairs right in an instant, cure the imbecile man at once, make a healthy artist of your consumptive daughter, and all such practical things. All these powers are natural, inherent, waiting to break forth as the morning. Only one door closes against them. That door is a false notion. Drop the false notion and the faculty is free in an instant, whether it is a hunch back, a short leg, or a congenital blindness. The saying, "I believe in universal freedom" will start you on the right road.

The peculiarity of the blind man at the temple gate was his obedient spirit. There were throngs of blind men at those gates, but Jesus Christ saw that one who was willing to be the laughing stock of a city street by running though it with two clots of mud on his face in obedience to the command of the only mind that carried any possible hope in its tones.

Obedience was his characteristic. They had told him that some of God's children must be beggars and he believed it. They told him he was blind, and he believed it. But he sprang like a bird from the snare of her fowlers when a loving heart said, "I deny these statements."

As an idea that gets possession has such remarkable effects, you had better be careful to get the idea of unlimited Good. You had better be meek enough to obey this law even though it be broached to you by a Christian scientist. Obedience to principle in spite of the comments of your neighbors will do as marvelous things for you as for this blind man.

"Who follow Truth though men deride,

In Her strength shall be strong;

Shall see their shame before their pride,

And share Her triumph song."

Martin Luther was of an obedient mind and so was chosen to be the reformer instead of the far abler Melanchthon. Melanchthon was more careful of "an intelligent public opinion." Saul of Tarsus was obedient to the highest idea he realized and so was chosen to convert the gentiles and preach the Holy Spirit. Remember that the "intelligent public" is never a friend to the seeker for Truth till after it has "thrust him out," as the Jews did this blind man, and his cause has worked like leaven to gain the respect and love of the bold and fearless.

Jesus here speaks of the necessity for works, or the significance they bear to the power of a man's doctrine. Such cases as this must not be going around, he said, "I must work the works of the Good." All healing by your doctrine is evidence of the spiritual power thereof. "While it is day," He said. He meant that span of duties laid in the pathway of all who are walking over this planet. Each one of us meets just such a set of affairs as we are perfectly capable of setting into right relations. We must not refuse any one of these duties. Do our highest best by every one of them, with no alighting of any task. Nothing is impossible. "As thy day is, so shall thy strength be." If you will take notice, the greatest foe your mind has in its realm is the belief in limitation. It is sometimes called doubt. Jesus Christ said He would do His faith-work, or show what an idea in faith would work, and then let their night-ways or doubt-ways deal with the world for a while.

It has been these night-ways or doubt-reign since the crucifixion, but now the morning of understanding breaks. Health springs forth speedily. Our joy no man taketh from us. Christ has come again. We will not believe that there is any power in an evil idea. We do not believe that God intended or permits blindness, pain, poverty. These things are but the false teachings of men who have insisted, as Beecher did, "suffering is a part of the divine idea." We hurl this lie from our mind, and lo, here is a new strength. Here is the ability to throw away our spectacles. They were only our externalization into works of our belief in suffering as part of God's plan.

Jesus Christ made clay and anointed the eyes. He took this same old curative preparation and made it work to show how it was the difference in His state of mind from theirs. They had used it many times on this same man while they believed in the law of sin and death as part of God's plan. He knew better, and His state of mind took the same stuff and had a different effect. Everything you touch will be successful when you drop your "son of perdition," or idea of the badness of God.

"Go wash," just as this blind man did; that is, deny or reject your old notions, "in the pool of Siloam," in the waters of pure Goodness.

"By cool Siloam's shady rill

How sweet the lily grows."

You are by nature the lily of Siloam. If you speak these words you will prove it; "I drop my belief in the law of sin."

Then when the blind man saw, they "put him out." Of course, "in the world ye shall have tribulation." But you are not expected to mix with the world. You are to triumph over every one of its beliefs by rejecting them, no matter if the greatest orators give them credence. *"I am the light of the world."* Any man who tells Truth is a light. Any man who announces a principle is a light.

You must announce five things with great vehemence. These they are:

God is the unending, changeless life of the universe.

God is the undefilable, unchanging health of the universe.

God is the unfailing, irresistible strength of the universe.

God is the unfailing, ever present support of the universe.

God is the immovable defense of the universe.

These principles have not been announced till now. They have always been hidden by the words, "death, disease, weakness, poverty, danger." A word is a great thing. "For the lightest word there is account." Keep these last words out of your vocabulary in simple mercy. Wash clean in the holy Siloam of these words:

I do not believe in an inheritance of sin. I do not believe in the race experience of sin. I do not believe in the contagion of sin. I do not believe in myself as a sinner. I believe I am a child of God.

"How sweet the lily grows." Now, you can deny blindness in the same washing words, can't you? Try it. No matter who taught you of an inheritance of failing vision, say, "I deny it."

Do you remember the prophecy John made, that the "old dragon" should be destroyed in the last days by the testimony of the saints? The old dragon is the belief in sin. You are one of the saints to stand before the throne and shout your testimony. "I testify that I know that God is all, and in Him is no darkness of sin." After the testimony the man was received into union with Christ by thinking the same thoughts Christ thought.

Think Plato's thoughts and get one cold mind with him. Think Aristotle and get away from home and honor with him. Think Jesus Christ and step into your Father's house. "Let the same mind be in you that was in Christ Jesus."

How? Why, by thinking His thoughts. He made no mistakes. Leave Fenelon, a Kempis, and Guyon out of your ideals. They believed in the atonement by suffering. They were mistaken. There is no suffering whatsoever connected with marriage with the Spirit.

Atonement is uniting or marriage. Be united to God only, the Holy Spirit. "Thy maker is thine husband." "I have set My Name upon thee." "I have espoused thee." "The Spirit and the bride say, come." Fold yourself round with the glory of Truth till you do not see any evil in all your universe, for you have given that testimony which has destroyed it, or rather has caused the eternal day of God to break over. See, the dark corners of earth wait your testimony.

Then thou shalt have no need of the sun, neither of the moon, to give light unto thee, for The Lord shall be thy everlasting light, and the days of thy mourning are ended, Testimony will break down the middle walls of partition and be an open sesame into this fair kingdom that lies around us. People have hidden God's kingdom by accusations against Him.

We make it visible by refusing to believe in those accusations. We take the words of Truth and are at one mind with God. "I and the Father are One."

September 13, 1891

Lesson XII

THE REAL KINGDOM

John 10:1-16

"He that entereth not by the door into the sheepfold — the same is a thief and a robber."

The "sheepfold" is the kingdom of heaven. The kingdom of heaven is not a place, though the place where we are may seem heavenly. The real kingdom of heaven is the right state of mind.

The right state of mind is where there is perfect health, perfect judgment, and perfect prosperity. These are all secured by right reasoning. The most exalted or freest reasoning gives the most exalted state of mind. If anybody stops short in his reasoning he stops short in his health and judgment — also in his prosperity.

The only way to get into heaven or a perfect state of mind is to reason to the highest ultimates your mind can conceive without regarding whether it would be considered *reductio ad absurdum* by the old-fashioned doctrines or not.

As everybody is trying to get into the "sheep-fold" here mentioned, let us consider "the door," or the doctrine taught by Jesus Christ so consistently that He called Himself "the Door."

We may readily conceive of ourselves as one with our doctrine, that we are it, if we have thought and taught and demonstrated it as Jesus Christ did His doctrine.

"The sheep" are your thoughts. The calling of your thoughts "sheep" is very appropriate, because thoughts are docile and obedient like sheep. You yourself are the keeper of your thoughts and lead them where you will.

Every obedient little idea has faithfully pictured that pink glow on your cheek, or that happy light in your eye. The thoughts referred to here are your thoughts of God, particularly, and what those thoughts do at all times.

There is one thought you have which you have always held strongly and definitely, or indifferently and indefinitely; it is the thought, "God is my friend."

If you started this thought long ago and held it warmly and confidently, you are a good friend to everybody and you now number among your comrades one warm, strong, efficient, unchangeable, loving friend. There is another thought which is of the obedient character of the sheep here meant. It is the idea that "God is omnipotent." This idea, held in confidence, has made you strong in yourself. The most obedient thoughts you have are your thoughts of God. Jesus, when speaking of sheep, refers entirely to ideas of God. It is ideas of God, which, if you shepherd well, will get you into that state of mind called heaven, when you have health, judgment, prosperity. Jesus Christ was sure that His doctrine was the door, and everybody else's the climbing in some other way. They had all before Him proved themselves thieves and robbers. Why? They had robbed men and women of health, judgment, and prosperity. Ninety years before Him there had ridden through the streets of Rome, Pompey, proclaimed conqueror of the whole world.

Nine hundred cities, 1000 castles, sacked; long lines of manacled captives, with heads hung low and speechless tongues, sightless eyes, broken hearts.

There was splendid triumph for Pompey and the nations shouted his greatness.

But Jesus Christ said that was not the doctrine that would make heaven manifest on the earth. His doctrine was the only "door." His doctrine would bind up the broken-hearted, loose the dumb tongues, unstop deaf ears, open blind eyes, lift up the cast-down heads. Not only that, but all over the universe you might look for captivity where His doctrine had been preached (or His door opened) and you would not find captivity itself for He had "led captivity captive."

Whoever has any bondage to anything whatsoever, believes more in Pompey's doctrine than in
Jesus Christ's. For Pompey believed in bondage,
but Jesus Christ believed in freedom. Jesus Christ
was sure He had the only doctrine that would set
absolutely free. A locksmith is sure he has the only
combination that will open the safe. If another
man has the same combination he can get in, oth-
erwise not. Jesus Christ knew His doctrine to be
the only door into safety.

A mother had a baby that she loved so much
she was like a barnacle to its little life. She felt
ownership, clinging fondness for it. So the baby
boy began to dwindle and pine away. Hungry love
always drives its object away. If you long after and
hunger for and eat with fondness in your affections, the object of your affections will take every
means to keep out of your way. So this little boy
was getting away in self-defense. No treatment
helped the puny child till the mother said over and
over in her heart: "You are God's child, you are
God's child."

She kept this up till she loosed the tentacles of
her mind off his life, and he sprang forth as free
and robust and hardy as a boy could be. This was
the door or teaching of Jesus. "One is your Father,
even God."

Is not that teaching theft and robbery, which
takes away sight, hearing, hopes?

Jesus Christ had nothing to say against
Pompey as a child of God, but his expecting to

enter into heaven by his beliefs was folly. Jesus explained that the porter at the door of heaven is the Holy Spirit. The true doctrine will bring you face to face with the Holy Spirit who will lead you into greater and greater knowledge. The Holy Ghost will teach you all things — guide you into all truth. Just as soon as you take the doctrine of Jesus — actually take it — there is a fall of sweet, loving power over all thought. Once you spoke carelessly, "I believe in God as my friend," but now you speak it in delightful assurance that "whatsoever things ye ask for ye shall have." Every friend who comes to you, you know very well that they are coming to you for your words about God. All truth about God brings good friends, good success.

Jesus Christ praises Himself as His doctrine, and praises His doctrine as Himself. He lives in blissful ignorance that there is any idea that His doctrine and Himself are not God.

When you praise yourself you begin to know yourself. Try it. Praise yourself silently at first, for you have not at first shown that your words are true by your works. Say, "I am wise. I am bold, I am good. I am able to do everything perfectly." You will soon show forth to all the world that you are indeed all this. Then you will have a beautiful effect upon the people. But, indeed:

"Thou must be true thyself

If Thou the Truth would teach;

Thy soul must overflow with, love.

Loving results to reach."

Now try once speaking some of Jesus Christ's doctrine. He set before you an open door which no man can shut (or no prejudice or fears of anybody keep you from getting the benefit of). Let all your thoughts lie still as the pool of Bethesda for a little while. Now, if your mind is quite placid stir it with this beautiful text: *"I am the resurrection and the life; he that believeth in Me though he were dead, yet shall he live again."*

He had unbounded confidence in Himself. You must have unbounded confidence in yourself. Your Father is the same one that Jesus Christ had. Your substance is exactly like His substance. Your powers are exactly like His. You have the same privilege to ignore your birth in the flesh that He had. You can demonstrate over hardship, pain, trouble, as well as He if you have His combination, or doctrine, or "door." When you have got His teachings truly, you will not follow after strange doctrines.

When you once have said, "I do not believe in the power of evil to come nigh my life," and somebody tells you your house and children are burned, you will boldly say: "I do not believe it."

Your calamities will turn out not calamities at all. The stronger you hold onto your words the nobler your blessings. After once saying, "Spirit is the only substance," nobody can make you believe that a whole tide of spirits exists.

After saying: "God is good; God is all," you would not credit the story of anybody who should say that in a vision he had a picture of hell. There would not be in your mind the slightest credence of the accuracy of that little girl's vision of Jesus Christ taking her by the hand to show her the sight of many people in hell. It would not be consistent with your knowledge of His saying that children's true thoughts always behold the good only.

He said He came with a teaching that would give life more and more abundantly. A woman's beloved husband lay dying (according to other men's opinions.) She knew that according to Jesus Christ he had a right to more abundant life. So she leaned hard on some words of Jesus Christ. These were "God is Love." She said them over and over and the air became vivified with Love. The man revived and lives, strong in God.

A man who felt himself ignorant got down on his face on the mountain side night after night, saying to the folding presence of God; "Thou knowest all things." He repeated the words often. Repetition of truth is the quickening. After some days he became very wise.

There was an extraordinary judgment and intelligence about the man. Whoever comes nearest to the principle of speech announced by Jesus Christ is really most successful in life. Life — such life as His words give — is miraculous. His words are pure reasoning. Be careful not to stop short on your reasonings along His lines, for that is to stop short in health, intelligence, prosperity.

Right reasoning leads you on to the topless heights of the hills of God, from whence cometh our help. The most exalted reasoning concerning yourself as the substance and manifestation of God is the most exalted reward. Where have you stopped in your reasoning? There where you have stopped is where old age begins to seize you, pain lays hold, sickness settles. You have a right to rise to the hills of glory on the wings of the words of Jesus. Speak these words of His: "I am the root and the offspring of David, and the bright and morning star."

See how hereby you announce yourself one with God in the beginning, now His manifestation by your word, and the shining glory of His goodness in the sight of all mankind, *"Heaven and earth shall pass away, but My words shall not pass away."*

September 20, 1891

I am all powerful.
I am in control of everything
that can affect me.
I am in total control of my
destiny.

Lesson XIII

IN RETROSPECTION

Review

Today we are requested to make a definite review of the lessons of the last quarter, remind the Christian believer of his duty as a missionary of his doctrine, and speak for practical temperance in the conduct and speech of the human race.

As one gets newer and newer ideas of a landscape by looking at it intently, so to look at a Bible text steadily, thinking it over carefully, we come to newer and newer revelations of its meanings.

So a review of the lessons of the last quarter will give us new spiritual insights.

Two ways of teaching the practice of divine principle have been in vogue; first, the statement of the whole doctrine in one short sentence, as in St. John 1, and then the particularization of that doctrine in living application, as in the statements following the first of John. The second method is the statement of particular cases and the explanation hereof according to universal principles, as a teacher might tell his pupil to take in, item by item, the views of his landscape and report the whole in the order of his survey.

The method of John concerning the meaning of Jesus and His principle is to say that *"In the beginning the Word was with God and the Word was God."*

God is the eternal Mind. Without Him was not anything made that was made.

The thought of a mind is its word. As the Word that filled the Mind of God was God, of course the Word was equal in presence, power, and knowledge with its Thinker, Whose Mind it absolutely occupied.

And John taught that this Word made all that was made.

Looking over the universe and seeing the earthquake swallowing its thousands, the tidal waves drowning cities, with the countless other manifestations of what does not coincide with this affirmation of John and Jesus and Moses — that all that the Word made was good — we find that an explanation of what they did indeed mean, is necessary.

Nobody can make us call earthquakes and pestilences good. "Woe unto them that call evil good."

Those who call calamity good always try to get away from it.

The martyrs who did not try to get away from persecution had their minds so filled with the name Jesus Christ that they did not notice what was going on around them. They did not explain that it was the absorption of their own mind with the name that gave them no room or space in mind for any other idea, that kept them from pain, but so it was.

One whose mind is absolutely occupied by an idea has no room for a thought of pain.

Now the Word that occupies the mind of God is God. And the creation of that Word is all good.

Paul says there is a veil over the eyes of those who read the Scriptures about God. This is because people have accused God of creating both good and evil, "As I live, saith the Lord, I know the thoughts that I think towards you; thoughts of peace and not of evil." The word satan held in mind steadily would make all things dark and horrible and ugly toward us. We would finally conclude with Schopenhauer that God, the ruling force of the universe, is gigantic evil evolving into good. It would not make it true, but would make everything hopelessly uncomfortable for us.

On the contrary, the word God held in mind will fill all things with glory and a noble ecstasy for us.

People have held in mind the words Holy Ghost, and the words Holy Spirit, till their mind was so renewed that their bodies were rejuvenated.

People have urged holding the mind to the words "praise God," because so many men and women with tangled business affairs have straightened them out so satisfactorily by looking them straight in the face and saying, "Praise God."

"With God all things are possible." The word God is the password into the kingdom of joy and gladness, God is Spirit. The word Spirit is the passport into substantial satisfaction. Not the word "spirits;" there are no spirits. There is one Spirit only — God.

John secondly bore record of Jesus Christ as the living demonstration of one who had held the word God in mind. He showed the way out of all the circumstances and conditions into which mankind has complicated itself by believing that God made evil as well as Good.

There is no failure of knowing exactly what to do when the mind is set free and made true and joyous by the true thought of God.

The Texas Compass plant always points truly north and south when it is not burdened with dust. Our judgment is perfectly true when one theme only occupies it.

"Thou art my theme, my inspiration, and my crown:

My strength in age, my pleasure, wealth — my world."

John tells, thirdly, that what no one could ever accomplish by practicing any external science, or even by faith, the good presence of God could be brought to pass instantly after the experience of the atonement — or at-oneness of the kind of man with the Mind that is God through thinking of God.

Jesus Christ took the six stone water-pots, representing the six ugly situations of the human lot, and filled them with rich wine to symbolize how the homeliest lot can be made joyously satisfactory by our being united to God in mind.

Jesus then explained to Nicodemus that the showing forth of the mind after it is sure of its oneness with God is so beautiful that it is like being born again.

The process of systematic thinking to cleanse and quicken the mind is called in the science of mind denial and affirmation. We deny the reality of the principle of evil, and affirm the good only as a principle of action. John tells how Jesus taught his lesson of rest after labor by walking the long journey towards Jacob's well and resting thereon. Almost everyone has some goal toward which his efforts are made. If he has done his best and the end seems as far from attainment as at first he must give it up — rest.

The time of discouragement and weariness and what seems failed hope is the time to give up and rest. Look for the sudden bloom of your hopes when you are willing to give up your hopes.

The best and the highest powers and words spring forth after letting go with the mind. After His rest He announced Himself as the Messiah, He called Himself the Well of Living Water. All who speak truthfully of their spiritual nature are found to radiate a peculiar refreshment and healing.

Take one who boldly announces himself as a believer in the unfailing bounty of God and you will find yourself suddenly devising wise ways and means for the management of your affairs while you are in his society. Take one who believes in God as his unfailing health and you will find in his society great impetus toward health. Take the one who announces that he believes in God as his unerring judgment and your own judgment will be nobler in his presence.

"I will tell you, Socrates, a thing incredible, yet nevertheless true, I made a great proficiency when I associated with you, when I was in the same house, though not in the same room."

The next lesson was for the instructing of us all out of the habit of self-condemnation. Self-condemnation leads to condemnation by other people who find fault with us.

We must take the good word into our mind that, "There is no condemnation."

Seventhly, John taught how Jesus fed multitudes with small visible resources simply by giving thanks and praising the Spirit of God for the law of the self-increasing potency of every substance. Take the few pennies or the small revenues you are possessed of and do likewise and you will surely see the increase.

Then John laid plainly before us that we must not believe in the necessity for hard work in order to live joyously. Also that we must give down our will into the Divine will by saying, "I came not to do mine own will," or else we would run our necks headstrong into great obligations and responsibilities.

He showed in the tenth that what we see in others is the sight of some word in our own mind, and our eyesight depends upon how we see people, whether spiritually born or carnally born.

Here also we discover the fact of the other seeing faculty once owned by the human race which now we are quickening again.

In the eleventh we are told to deny reincarnation and the heredity of sin.

Twelfthly, he proves by the results of the teachings of Jesus we may see that His doctrine is the only door into satisfactory living.

The lesson on missionary work shows that no matter if the Red Sea of difficulty seems to lie in our path, we are to preach the gospel we know to be true.

The temperance lesson opened up to us the joyous information that no man ever wanted strong drink. He wants only strong words. When those are given the rum appetite is gone. Temperance means good judgment. Even children love good judgment. They naturally have it. But if somebody tells a child that he does not know what he is about, or fears all the time that he will do something wrong, his sweet, true judgment is hidden, and he goes seeking among tobaccos and cards for his hidden faculty. Whoever would set him free must praise the hidden judgment till it springs forth a glorious goodness; not for anything describe the poor judgment with which the Divine is covered.

A child that is told of "spirits" loses judgment or rather has it hidden. There is only one Spirit. "Do not I fill heaven and earth?" To tell a drinker of ardent spirits there is but one Spirit; even though you tell him silently, will "satisfy his soul in thought," while "describing his evil case" will be your accusing.

You remember that John the Revelator saw four angels (accusing words) given power to hurt the earth.

But other angels sealed the servants of the Living God in their foreheads to keep them from the four accusations.

The four accusations against God's people are that: first, they are liars; second, they are unsound; third, that they have wicked propensities; and fourth, that they are made of a dying substance called mortality. If the beautiful temperance women would spend their generous

110

energies speaking to and of the living goodness of the soul that the accusers have hidden, the goodness of mankind would break forth as the morning,

"I, Jesus, have sent mine angel to testify that this is true."

September 27,1891

.

Notes

Other Books by Emma Curtis Hopkins

- *Class Lessons of 1888 (WiseWoman Press)*
- *Bible Interpretations (WiseWoman Press)*
- *Esoteric Philosophy in Spiritual Science (WiseWoman Press)*
- *Genesis Series*
- *High Mysticism (WiseWoman Press)*
- *Self Treatments with Radiant I Am (WiseWoman Press)*
- *Gospel Series (WiseWoman Press)*
- *Judgment Series in Spiritual Science (WiseWoman Press)*
- *Drops of Gold (WiseWoman Press)*
- *Resume (WiseWoman Press)*
- *Scientific Christian Mental Practice (DeVorss)*

Books about Emma Curtis Hopkins and her teachings

- *Emma Curtis Hopkins, Forgotten Founder of New Thought –
  Gail Harley*
- *Unveiling Your Hidden Power: Emma Curtis Hopkins' Meta-
  physics for the 21st Century (also as a Workbook and as A
  Guide for Teachers) – Ruth L. Miller*
- *Power to Heal: Easy reading biography for all ages –Ruth
  Miller*

To find more of Emma's work, including some previously unpublished material, log on to:

www.emmacurtishopkins.com

WISEWOMAN PRESS

1521 NE Jantzen Ave #143
Portland, Oregon 97217
800.603.3005
www.wisewomanpress.com

Books Published by WiseWoman Press

By Emma Curtis Hopkins

- *Resume*
- *Gospel Series*
- *Class Lessons of 1888*
- *Self Treatments including Radiant I Am*
- *High Mysticism*
- *Esoteric Philosophy in Spiritual Science*
- *Drops of Gold Journal*
- *Judgment Series*
- *Bible Interpretations: series I, II and III*

By Ruth L. Miller

- *Unveiling Your Hidden Power: Emma Curtis Hopkins' Metaphysics for the 21st Century*
- *Coming into Freedom: Emily Cady's Lessons in Truth for the 21st Century*
- *150 Years of Healing: The Founders and Science of New Thought*
- *Power Beyond Magic: Ernest Holmes Biography*
- *Power to Heal: Emma Curtis Hopkins Biography*
- *The Power of Unity: Charles Fillmore Biography*
- *Uncommon Prayer*
- *Spiritual Success*
- *Finding the Path*

Watch our website for release dates and order information! - www.wisewomanpress.com

List of
Bible Interpretation Series
with date from 1st to 14th series.

This list is complete through the fourteenth Series. Emma produced at least thirty Series of Bible Interpretations.

She followed the Bible Passages provided by the International Committee of Clerics who produced the Bible Quotations for each year's use in churches all over the world.

Emma used these for her column of Bible Interpretations in both the Christian Science Magazine, at her Seminary and in the Chicago Inter-Ocean Newspaper.

First Series

Second Series

Third Series

Fourth Series

April 3 - June 26, 1892

Fifth Series

Sixth Series

Seventh Series

January 1 - March 31, 1893

Lesson 1	All is as Allah Wills	January 1st
	Ezra 1	
	Khaled Knew that he was of The Genii	
	The Coming of Jesus	
Lesson 2	Zerubbabel's High Ideal	January 8th
	Ezra 2:8-13	
	Fulfillments of Prophecies	
	Followers of the Light	
	Doctrine of Spinoza	
Lesson 3	Divine Rays Of Power	January 15th
	Ezra 4	
	The Twelve Lessons of Science	
Lesson 4	Visions Of Zechariah	January 22nd
	Zechariah 3	
	Subconscious Belief in Evil	
	Jewish Ideas of Deity	
	Fruits of Mistakes	
Lesson 5	Aristotle's Metaphysician	January 27th
	Missing (See Review for summary)	
Lesson 6	The Building of the Temple	February 3rd
	Missing (See Review for summary)	
Lesson 7	Pericles and his Work in building the Temple	
	Nehemiah 13	February 12th
	Supreme Goodness	
	On and Upward	
Lesson 8	Ancient Religions	February 19th
	Nehemiah 1	
	The Chinese	
	The Holy Spirit	
Lesson 9	Understanding is Strength Part 1	February 26th
	Nehemiah 13	
Lesson 10	Understanding is Strength Part 2	March 3rd
	Nehemiah 13	
Lesson 11	Way of the Spirit	March 10th
	Esther	
Lesson 12	Speaking of Right Things	March 17th
		Proverbs 23:15-23
Lesson 13	Review	March 24th

Eighth Series

April 2 - June 25, 1893

Lesson 1   The Resurrection   April 2nd
                      Matthew 28:1-10
                      One Indestructible
                      Life In Eternal Abundance
                      The Resurrection
                      Shakes Nature Herself
                      Gospel to the Poor

Lesson 2   Universal Energy   April 9th
                      Book of Job, Part 1

Lesson 3   Strength From Confidence   April 16th
                      Book of Job, Part II

Lesson 4   The New Doctrine Brought Out   April 23rd
                      Book of Job, Part III

Lesson 5   The Golden Text   April 30th
                      Proverbs 1:20-23
                      Personification Of Wisdom
                      Wisdom Never Hurts
                      The "Two" Theory
                      All is Spirit

Lesson 6   The Law of Understanding   May 7th
                      Proverbs 3
                      Shadows of Ideas
                      The Sixth Proposition
                      What Wisdom Promises
                      Clutch On Material Things
                      The Tree of Life
                      Prolonging Illuminated Moments

Lesson 7   Self-Esteem   May 14th
                      Proverbs 12:1-15
                      Solomon on Self-Esteem
                      The Magnetism of Passing Events
                      Nothing Established by Wickedness
                      Strength of a Vitalized Mind
                      Concerning the "Perverse Heart"

Ninth Series

July 2 - September 27, 1893

Lesson 1	Secret of all Power	July 2nd
Acts 16: 6-15	The Ancient Chinese Doctrine of Taoism	
	Manifesting of God Powers	
	Paul, Timothy, and Silas	
	Is Fulfilling as Prophecy	
	The Inner Prompting.	
	Good Taoist Never Depressed	
Lesson 2	The Flame of Spiritual Verity	July 9th
Acts 16:18	Cause of Contention	
	Delusive Doctrines	
	Paul's History	
	Keynotes	
	Doctrine Not New	
Lesson 3	Healing Energy Gifts	July 16th
Acts 18:19-21	How Paul Healed	
	To Work Miracles	
	Paul Worked in Fear	
	Shakespeare's Idea of Loss	
	Endurance the Sign of Power	
Lesson 4	Be Still My Soul	July 23rd
Acts 17:16-24	Seeing Is Believing	
	Paul Stood Alone	
	Lessons for the Athenians	
	All Under His Power	
	Freedom of Spirit	
Lesson 5	(Missing) Acts 18:1-11	July 30th
Lesson 6	Missing No Lesson *	August 6th
Lesson 7	The Comforter is the Holy Ghost	August 13th
Acts 20	Requisite for an Orator	
	What is a Myth	
	Two Important Points	
	Truth of the Gospel	
	Kingdom of the Spirit	
	Do Not Believe in Weakness	

125

126

Tenth Series

Twelfth Series

April 1 – June 24, 1894

Thirteenth Series

July 1 – September 30, 1894

Fourteenth Series

October 7 – December 30, 1894